Management Done Right

Management Done Right

The Massive Difference between **Logical** and **Emotional** Management

HAROLD SMART

ISBN: 978-1-4834-9472-2 (sc)
ISBN: 978-1-4834-9474-6 (hc)
ISBN: 978-1-4834-9473-9 (e)

Library of Congress Control Number: 2018914360

Lulu Publishing Services rev. date: 01/23/2019

Contents

Foreword

Corporate structure stifles creativity, decreases productivity and maintains the status quo, but why does this occur? This is the question that Management Done Right tries to answer in a witty, comical nature. Mr. Smart is a keen observer of others which is clear in his description of the companies and specific people with whom he worked. Part historian, part manager, and just a bit irreverent, this book tackles the complacency and reasons why so many businesses fail as they get larger. Small companies always want to get bigger, but as they do, they follow the model of those same companies they left to start their own company leading to frustration of independent and creative workers.

This book is fun to read, and everyone will see at least one of their managers within the pages. Thoughtful leaders will also see themselves and a few ideas of how to prevent the traps which are so easy to fall into. Perhaps you will determine that you will choose the unconventional but ultimately much more satisfying way to lead. Perhaps you will learn which types of companies you want to avoid and what the warning signs are if you work in mid-sized companies. No matter your background, this book is sure to give you more than a few laughs and challenge your thoughts about leadership.

Reading this together with your peers may be the best way to enjoy this book. What was each person's take away with each chapter? What could be changed in your own organization to help dismantle the current structure and create a more nimble and creative workplace? If company resources are being abused, is it better to create rules or just move the offending parties out the door? How do you create an atmosphere where everyone feels empowered to state their true feedback and ideas?

All companies struggle with these questions, but most companies follow the same playbook. Mr. Smart calls for new thoughts and ideas which will challenge us and break down some of the barriers for growth. He does this by pointing out some of the crazy, funny and, unfortunately, ubiquitous maladaptive behaviors corporate America has developed. Anyone who has worked in a company with over 50 people will enjoy this look at the corporate structure.

Sincerely,
Robin Germany, MD

1: Boiling Over

Complainers. Criticizers. Blamers. Idiots. Slick BS artists. No guts or can-do in any of them. No wonder it took me longer to unwind after leaving the corporate world than it did after I returned from Vietnam. Now, I know I'm wired a little differently, but surely I'm not the only one who can see that most companies succeed in spite of themselves instead of because of themselves. Surely I'm not the only one who can see that a corporation's life span is on a very predictable path, a very obvious life cycle. If you know what you're looking for. Apparently most people don't know what to look for. They can't see how the actions that the influential people take, the choices they make, are just perpetuating the nonsense that leads to the death of a company. Oftentimes it's a very long, slow, and painful one.

I was in my truck, and the events of the day running through my mind were just serving to frustrate me. I had to pull off to the side of the road. Grabbing the nearest pen and scrap of paper, I started to write. "Cumulative effect of obstructions in business, any one alone may not be catastrophic, but too many of them is a killer." "The only constant is change. The ability to see opportunities and adapt to ever changing conditions is essential and something rigid people and companies can't do." "Typical flaws in management: questionable training, no training, Peter Principle, pets, bullies, college degrees only, add up to impeding the work that needs to be done. What happened, and happens, to good managers?"

That wasn't all. There was more. Much more. It was just a jumble of words and phrases, but I felt a little better after letting off some steam.

As I stared down at this random list, though, I realized a few things. The first was that my handwriting wasn't easy to read. Second, as I skimmed through these notes again, I realized that these thoughts had been gnawing on me for years. Like a pot too long over a flame, these ideas were starting to boil over. The industry I'm in has recently been completely disrupted. Buyouts, mergers, some companies changing owners a couple of times in the space of a few months. What's going on, and where will it end?

The same basic theories are used all over the corporate world, the same basic tenants of business and bureaucracy. When one business fails, another swoops in to take it over or tear it to pieces. Yet, they are using the same model as the failed business. Does it never occur to the new owners that the same thing will happen to them a few years down the road? I guess not because they just keep doing the same thing over and over, copying the plan that, as proven by the last company that went under, doesn't work. Oftentimes only the logo remains—a sad testament to the reality I was beginning to see. Most of those "me too" companies, the large ones, ended up with a typical corporate management structure before being absorbed or shut down.

Most people think this is the price of progress and the global economy, but I call BS. I think people just get so caught up that they don't realize they're running their company the way most others are. They keep doing what they're doing because they don't stop to think that it might not be the best way or that there might be another. Some just don't want to take the risk of changing the system. Everyone else does it that way! The devil you know…

When I got back on the road that day, my mind didn't stop. Now that I'd started thinking about the corporate structure, patterns began to emerge, and I began to see a model used by most corporations I'd observed. One that was seriously flawed.

Those notes were only the beginning. It definitely wasn't the last time I pulled over to the side of the road to write out more notes on the hilarious and, oftentimes, downright foolish practices of corporate America. By the time I considered writing a book, I had pages and pages.

Now, you might be wondering who I am, and, perhaps, why you should listen to anything I have to say. Don't worry. I'm not offended. I'm ready and willing to answer those questions.

I grew up on a subsistence farm just outside a small town in Northeastern Oklahoma where there was little money and, sometimes, little food and clothing. It plugged one into reality real quick. I started working for hire, running a paper route, when I was 13. Our family did custom hay hauling during the summer months, so I worked doing that as well. In high school, I was often in charge of 1-3 trucks and from 1-8 workers ranging from overgrown 13 year-old boys to 50 year-old men. Because my father's health prevented him from doing the work, he took care of business and errands while I took care of the field.

When everyone who works for you is bigger and stronger than you are, you don't "boss" them around. You lead. (By the time I was a senior in high school, I was 5'10' but only 135 lbs—not intimidating in the least.) To get them to work, I had to earn their respect by knowing my job and teaching them the easiest way to handle hay bales. It was hard work, and the turnover rate was high. Average time a hand stayed on was no more than a week. We had a couple who stayed up to 2 weeks, but we also had those who only lasted half a day before the heat and work was too much. It was my first experience of managing, and I learned a lot about people and how to efficiently coordinate them to accomplish a task. You got your hands dirty, you earned their respect, and you paid them a fair wage. Simple.

I started college with only enough money for one semester's tuition and fees and the first month's room and board. I worked my way through the first three years of college. After that, I took a break from school and worked as a production machinist for a couple of years and served a three year term in the Army Special Forces with postings to Germany and Vietnam. Following my term in the Army, I immediately returned to college and finished my bachelor's degree.

I've been involved in operating several small businesses over the years, one of which I had owned with my brother-in-law. He had an opportunity to open a new service station in a mid-sized town. He had the financial backing, and I had experience with auto mechanics. We took the business off the ground, so to speak. We stocked the shelves, bought tools, and opened up for business. The location was projected to be selling 20,000 gallons of gasoline a month in 3-5 years. A competitor whose lot bordered on ours on the east side told us we wouldn't last 6 months. We put them out of business in 6 months instead. We focused on customers and their needs, and we hustled. Our station was new, and we kept it that way. At the end of the first year, we were selling 30,000 gallons of gas a month.

After that, I spent eleven years working for a manufacturing company that employed 1,000 people. It went from raw material, through fabrication, and marketed directly to hardware stores in all 50 states. My first 3 years were in the personnel department. The remaining 8 years was spent managing sales to other manufacturers. The objective was to sell available machine capacity from their aluminum extrusion machines to other manufacturers in the form of custom shapes. (The extrusion process is similar to squeezing material from a tube of toothpaste. You force the aluminum through a steel plate that has the cross section of a shape cut through it. Angles, bars, or any number of special shapes like aluminum window frame material. The aluminum is squirted out in long lengths, say 125 feet, then cut to workable lengths. This material is then sold to other manufacturers who used it to make their products.) My division, which was just a secretary clerk and myself, handled hundreds of accounts and grossed around $3M in sales annually. These came from large corporations all the way down to one person companies. This involvement with such a diverse variety of companies was some of the best experience I've had. During my time with this company, I attended night school and earned my MBA.

Following that, I ended up in an oil field production chemicals company with most of the market being small producers. In the first 32 years, the company I worked for never had a marketing effort. The reason we grew was because our competitors were not doing their job, and they would run business to us about as fast as we wanted to take it. The company grew from 6 employees to 170 by the time we were purchased by a large corporation.

Following that buyout a few years ago, I found myself back in the corporate world. I began to question the corporate model and the fact that those trapped in it have no idea what is happening to them.

Over the years, most of my job, whatever it happened to be at the time, has really been about problem solving. It's been my policy, as it is with most people who spend their lives fixing things, not to copy that which doesn't and can't work. Why would you? That doesn't make any sense. Whatever you're trying to fix won't get fixed. It might be a little less broken, if you're lucky, but it still won't work like it should.

In my years in and out of the corporate world and dealing with companies of all sizes, I've learned a thing or two about what works in a company and what doesn't. Building a strong, successful business takes more than time or money. It takes courage and a persistence to do it right. Over the years, I've seen and studied a whole lot of ways that people do it wrong and actually witnessed a few times that it was done right.

I'm under no illusions here. I have considered the possibility that people are going to toss aside the book without a thought, dismissing it as old-fashioned or missing the point. I've considered that it might make people angry because it might hit too close to home. I've considered those things and many more. Options considered, I felt it was time, past time really, that someone questioned the system, questioned the reason for copying the current management practices that don't make sense, can't work, and are pulling so many companies under. I felt that it was time that someone offered an alternative. There is one. Most people just don't know it.

I'm going to share the insights I've received over years of observation. This book uses my experience as a baseline, but I've had input from other sources as well, people like me who've seen firsthand the ridiculous, detrimental things that companies do. This is a collaborative effort, even though it's written in first person. The objective is to illustrate what is wrong with the prevailing management model, the foolishness of the current management theory, and to offer a superior alternative. No attempt is made to cover all the bases. You can't condense advanced degrees in business or years of experience into a few pages.

I am going to lay out the profile of a typical corporation and how it functions and malfunctions. I'm going to go over the human practices that cause things to fail, and to succeed, some of the personality types that typically contribute to the problems and those that contribute to the solutions. This isn't a touchy, feely, do-goody approach to management book. I'm not going to talk about sensitivity retreats and free cupcakes for the office to make people like you and/or do what you say. I'm going to talk about profit. It's an absolute necessity, not a dirty word. Without it, none of us would be employed. I'm going to talk about ambition. Again, it's not a dirty word. When channeled in a positive manner, it can make a great impact on the workplace. I am going to talk about managing, and I am going to talk about leadership.

Just a note of warning. I feel no obligation to do something a certain way just because it's always been done that way. That includes the writing of this book. I will have considered this venture a success if I can help save a company or, at the very least, make someone stop, think, and evaluate what they're doing in their company. I'm not going to use flowery words and diplomatic phrasing to convince you. I'm going to talk just like I would if we were having a cup of coffee together. You're going to need your sense of humor. Keep it handy.

Part 1
The Corporate Model

2: The Life Cycle

Most sizable companies follow what might be called "the corporate model". It is actually a copy of what appears to be the internal workings of a corporation. On paper it can be laid out in a logical form. Top manager, sub-managers of various functions such as sales, accounting, production, shipping, etc. Below these are several layers of management, and under them are the hourly employees. If you stopped and asked ten people from different levels of ten different corporations how a corporation should be run, you could get several different answers.

When a corporation fails, no one wants to take the time to search for the true cause of failure. They are content saying that the company mishandled funds, the employees didn't follow procedure, the market crashed under them. There are dozens, perhaps hundreds, of lame excuses. Ignorantly accepting such excuses without digging into the true cause is very shortsighted. I'm sure CEOs of other companies just tell their staff, and themselves, that it isn't going to happen to them. After all, they're going to run things tighter, more carefully than so-and-so other corporation. The fact is, though, that they usually end up doing the same things, and they don't even know it.

Now, I'm sure some people would say that the rise and fall of corporations is a good thing, that it does wonders for the economy, that it's important for competition in the marketplace, or some such other ridiculous nonsense. The reason the business was started, however, was to fill a need and make a profit doing it. It was started to succeed, not die a horribly ugly death. (A note here: The orientation of this book is for a company selling products along with technical support on how best to use those products, because that's what I know; however, much of it can be generalized to other markets.)

It would take a good, hard look, a heavy dose of courage, and an open mind for top management to stop and think that a corporation doesn't have to go the same way as any other. They might be able see that they are falling into the same pattern as all the rest, that their company is stuck in the same life cycle. There are many variations in the details of each company, but I've observed, and experienced, that the following model holds true in most cases.

A company starts for any number of reasons. A person just wants to be their own boss. Someone discovers a market that no one else has yet. Sometimes the business a person was employed by closes down for one reason or another, and they decide to pick up where that company left off. Employees of a large company are dissatisfied with their current place of employment (because of how the company treats their people, because the company doesn't take care of their customers, because the bureaucracy is just plain dumb, or one of a dozen other reasons), and they take their know-how and start a competing business. In any case, there is some sort of market vacuum. Nature abhors a vacuum, and something will get sucked in. A new business starts. It's the beginning of the cycle.

Most new companies struggle the first two years. It's just a fact. Even if the concept is a good one, and they treat their employees and customers right, it still takes time to get going. If the company makes it past that initial period of struggle and begins to put money on the bottom line, great. They're growing now. At this stage, many companies choose to continue on as a "small business." It's usually a good place to work and satisfying for the owner and their family for a few generations before it closes down or is sold. Some companies, however, choose to expand. That kind of growth is a risk, and not all choose to do it. If they succeed in their expansion goals, they are on their way to a higher degree of financial success.

The newly expanded company operates well for several years and continues to grow. The long-term employees have a loyalty to the founder that shows up in quality work and profit on the bottom line. It can be a really great place to work. The time span of this period often depends on the original owner's age and involvement.

A few years down the road, the original owner is getting older and starting to think about retiring. He can sell, shut down, or pass the reins to the next generation. (A note here: few companies survive a second generation and almost none make it through a third.) Whatever his decision, after it is made, he is not the only one who ends up leaving the company around that time. Key people leave or retire. Sometimes because it's time, sometimes because their health requires it, or sometimes just because they can't stand to work under their new boss. You can almost guarantee that these people won't be replaced with people of like mind or experience.

At the apex of the earning curve, then, things start to go wrong, and the profit margin starts declining. The new owner (new as in not the original even if the "new" one has been there a few years) starts looking for reasons, desperately searching for the answer to the dropping profits. There are literally hundreds of thousands of pages of advice on what to do, but none of them, seemingly, have been successful in preventing the eventual demise of most companies. The owner can follow the advice of others and bring in "new blood," or he can turn to his current management staff for answers. Anything to keep the business out of the red. Remember, though, that the management staff is "new" as well following the exodus after the original owner retired. Regrettably, these managers often have their own agenda, one unrelated to increasing the profitability of the business. This pushes the company further down this predictable path.

Under this, usually, aggressive management, things do change, but not necessarily for the best. Profit will start to even out, perhaps even increase for now, so the owner doesn't realize that the seeds of decline have been planted and are already growing. The amount of control the new management has put in place, the new edicts, the cuts in the budget for research and development, advertising, etc. all that begins to add up. Lethargy begins to take over, and the environment of the workplace declines as well. Over time, response to market begins to decline and other signs of the underlying stagnation begin to appear. The black ink on the bottom line steadily declines again, and it's a constant struggle to keep it from going red once more.

Management then goes on a cost savings rampage (pointing fingers the whole time). They always cut at the bottom where they are already threadbare on personnel and morale. You almost never see a VP give up 1 or 2 of their 8 secretaries. Accounting and engineering can't give up any people, whether those people are actually adding significant value to the company or just doing a bunch of busywork that serves little to no purpose. It goes that way through all the levels of the company. Whoever has the most power gets to keep all of their "serfs," thus demonstrating how much power they have.

Everyone in the office scrambles to head off any cuts in their departments. Order processing is already short handed, marketing can't let anyone go and still function, human resources is absolutely essential so you can't cut there! These managers are in the office daily and plead their cases well. Where can you cut? With a little thought, it's obvious to those on the outside of the big black box, as I "affectionately" call the corporate structure, where cuts should be made. That's not going to happen, though. Instead, the upper management issues orders to the middle management to lay off X number of people under them. Those in upper management won't have to look any of those people in the eye, so it doesn't affect them in any way, so they think. Wrong. They just fired a whole bunch of people who do the actual work that feeds the company. It will affect the entire organization. It's a damage over time effect. By the time they realize that something is amiss, it's too late.

I have seen cases where the field workers, we'll say 7 people, are doing 9 people's jobs. The office doesn't care. They tell the field manager he has to cut 4 workers. But! Don't have problems or let production suffer! Know what happens? The field manager tries to do the impossible, having 3 people do the job of 9, because he has no other option. Chances are good, and getting better by the day, that the hourly people will burn out and quit. Good workers are always scarce, and they won't be on the job market more than a few days before they go back to work someplace. When that starts, the field managers sometimes call corporate and tell them they're leaving their company vehicle at the yard and their keys on the desk. Just mail them their last check.

At this point, the corporation has crossed the great divide, and it's all downhill from there. The owners are faced with unpleasant choices. Shut down, file bankruptcy, pass the reins, or sell. Passing the reins will usually only prolong the agony of the company. If the owner chooses to sell, that sale will follow one of a few predictable paths. Sometimes corporate raiders buy them or gain stock control to sell disposable assets and dump what's left on the market for whatever they can get. Sometimes the company merges with another, bigger, company and the original company disappears entirely.

As long as it's not the case of corporate raiders, the owner is usually told that the buyer doesn't plan on changing anything. That turns out to be an untruth. They capitalize on the owner's desperation, or maybe they just think they're smarter, who knows. In any case, as soon as the ink dries, the changes start. They'll go through the company, cutting people they think they don't need. They'll keep the "sharpest people," aka the ones who tell them what they want to hear. These are, all too often, not your most productive employees, and some of them are outright liabilities. They can't see that. Over a period of a few months, they'll get rid of those they aren't impressed with.

A few years after the buyout, usually much sooner, most companies will bear little resemblance to the one that was sold, and the one that bought them will have little to show for the purchase. Total sales will not have increased as expected. They, somehow, don't manage to increase their market share or get into a new market. The end result is that there are no winners but a lot of losers.

The people with the most potential have been pushed out the door. This is a tremendous loss to the company. Not just in quality workers. They've also created some tough competition. The managers and CEOs are all deluded, thinking they are in control. If there are more than 20 employees on the payroll, then true control is usually an illusion. The bigger the organization, the more the bureaucracy controls it. The more they try to control it, the more rules-bound it becomes. From a company rules and regulations viewpoint, everything may be correct; however, nothing gets done in a timely or logical manner. All too often, nothing is done. Necessary work is ignored until it goes away, or it bounces from one department or manager to another until it is forgotten or lost.

Now the big company is not taking care of business, and they create a market vacuum. The same vacuum that started the process in the first place. Now we're full circle. One of those disgruntled employees will probably start their own business. He knows his former employer's business inside and out, and he knows how to exploit it's shortcomings. It's going to hurt. He can beat them with short response times and adaptability to market needs, and he can underbid with prices they can't match because he isn't paying for a lot of dead weight and inertia.

The new company expands, and the big company shrinks. Response at the big company is anger and desperation, just like what was happening at the smaller company it absorbed. They start badgering customers or cutting prices. This can speed up their demise, or it make their death that much slower and more painful, depending on circumstances. Customers will want to know why they can cut prices now in response to competition but couldn't have fair prices before being forced. They may feel betrayed, as may any long-term employees that are left. Top management already has their golden parachutes ready. Corporate assets are sold to prop things up a while longer. Eventually the name and an empty shell will go on the market. Some even bigger fish swallows them up, and, a couple of years later, no one will remember them.

An example of this. The company I worked for for 11 years was well run up to the 11th year. That year a group from the outside started a take over. They managed to get hired as the top management team. Like I said, few companies make it through a second generation. This was on its third and ripe for the picking. The company was very profitable at this time. Exactly how profitable was not widely known because it was a privately held company; being in middle management, however, I had a very good idea.

The first outsider persuaded the 3rd generation owners that they needed his expertise to make the company bigger and better. Once on board, he started adding his people into the top slots. Sales manager, product development, production, etc. These people were slick, dressed the part, and had a ready answer for every question. What the owner didn't realize was that these people all had agendas not related to the company's benefit. All of them loved power and felt superior to anyone not in their group. Anything or anyone that didn't reinforce their self-image did not last long.

As soon as they gained effective control, changes were made quickly. A special meeting was set up for all the department managers in the plant. Some of the managers were bought out with packages, some were forced to retire early, some were just let go. Of twenty-two managers, only 5 were left. The plan was to get rid of the higher salaries and move their lead men up because they could be paid much less. Not all of those lead men were capable of running a department. (The people they pushed out in this bloodbath were all top quality and were worth every penny they were paid.) To round things out, they called all the plant hourly employees into a meeting and informed them that they could be replaced by people from skid row. They stopped hiring and used only temps from temporary employee services. They now had cheap labor. They eliminated a lot of bookkeeping and benefits. And any regard for the workers as people.

The result? These "experts" operated the company to the very edge of bankruptcy. Twice. They managed to save it the last time by selling their most profitable single line to a large national company, then producing the products for them, under contract, with the same equipment. The top dog of this group was finally forced out, but most of the other top managers have hung on. I left before the bloodbath started because I knew where things were going. It was a cycle I was very familiar with, because I had watched dozens of companies go through similar transitions.

Morbid as it sounds, this is a fairly typical life cycle of a corporation (a death spiral, really). Response to customers becomes irrelevant. The company has the attitude that people will buy from them just because of their name. Their offices are full of people doing busywork to get a paycheck but who are rarely doing anything that contributes to the profitability of the company. Based on my observations, this happens in excess of 70% of the time in companies. Few of any size survive unscathed for 50 years.

What happened? Cancer. The symptoms were either ignored or were covered with a blue bandage. Top management and the board of directors sat on their butts and allowed disease to ravage the company. How? Why? Every department was run by the book. The same book, with the same methods, that nearly all large corporations follow, the one that most colleges, consultants, and trainers use. Do they ever stop to think the book might be wrong? Apparently not. No corporate management sees that the company survives as long as it does in spite of itself not because of itself.

That's just an overview of a corporation's life cycle. We're about to get into the details and specifics about the kinds of things that lead to collapse, the day to day workings that get bogged down in the mire of the bureaucracy.

3: No Risk, No Reward

Imagine the corporation as a big black box, sitting on 4 or 5 acres, several stories tall with no windows.

Inside the box is supposed to be everything necessary to operate efficiently. All managers and all employees are, additionally, fitted into nice neat little boxes of their own. I say "fitted," but I really mean forced, often messily with much crunching and lots of disgusting squishing noises. This ensures total control of all aspects of business. The manager's boxes are arranged in a pyramid, still inside the box, peaking out with a single CEO. The number of layers correspond to the number of other managers that can be controlled and spreads out to form the base. Each manger has hourly people working under them. That number is based on total control of their box people. You don't want to overload a manager, so you keep adding layers until all the boxes (aka hourly employees) can be properly micromanaged. You have to pay for all this, so you sell a product, a service, or a combination of the two. This is supposed to bring in enough money, through a very small door in the back at ground level, to support the interior of the entire box.

A little humor here. I was trying to think of what this model resembled, to what I could compare it. Then it hit me. What is everyone in the business world, well most every part of the world actually, always complaining about and bad-mouthing because of its lethargy and complete lack of efficiency? A government bureaucracy. A corporation and a government bureaucracy are extremely similar. The primary difference between the two is that a corporation is supposed to make a profit! Most people think of

17

the corporate model as a fairly recent development. It's not. The Egyptians and Greeks had highly developed bureaucracies which combined business and government functions. Oh. Did I mention the Romans… Why didn't this nice, neat arrangement work? Everything in the model is geared to be a stumbling block or a brick wall to getting anything accomplished. Most are quite proficient at it. But all in the name of efficiency, of course.

Every corporation has many layers of management. Too many layers of management. Many might rush to justify the reasons for them. After all, when a new problem arises, one that's never been addressed before, you might need a new layer, a new kind, of management to deal with it. That is the way most people think. Harsh as it sounds, stacked management kills an organization. These layers are a roadblock for getting anything useful done. Especially since you usually find 6 or 8 layers where 3 will do.

Let's say a request for an expenditure hits the bottom layer of management. Most of the time, nothing can be done. They can't spend the money they need to in order to get the job done. Upper management will not give those in the lower levels the power to make decisions of this nature. Perhaps because it will diminish their own power or because they simply don't trust those in their lower levels of management to be smart enough to spend money wisely. Whatever the reason, the request has to go up to the next layer of management which could, in theory, make a decision to get the work done. It won't happen. These people will recognize the risk involved in making a decision and pass it up the chain of command. The next person will recognize the risk and gladly send the request on to the next person, whoever corporate policy dictates that is. From here up to the top, everyone is playing the corporate game. They aren't going to risk their careers over this, whatever it is (they don't really know, and they don't care at all). They know that it doesn't matter what they've done for the company or how much they've contributed, they could get fired if this decisions costs the company at all. There are no rewards for taking risks and achieving, only punishment for failure, real or perceived, and they're not taking that chance.

For the sake of this explanation we'll say that the request continues up through the pyramid. No one rejects the request or pretends it got lost. It doesn't come back down with a request for more information before it has to travel back up again. It will eventually (and by eventually, I mean that it's already way past the time they lost some business because of it, they just don't know it) get to the person who has no choice but to respond to it. He doesn't want to make a decision. He might be wrong. He needs to cover his a**. What happens? He talks to a few other managers, and they form a committee. After all, they need to discuss the request (aka spread the risk). Doing this is safe, it protects a lot of people, and that is what they're concerned with: keeping what they have, no matter what the actual cost is down the line. Keeping the corporation profitable by taking some necessary risk is not their concern.

The committee doesn't have to be formal. A true example to give you an idea of this. A salesman called in to get pricing for a product around 9 a.m. He was told they'd get back with him. Around 2 p.m., he called again and learned that two other managers had been consulted but no consensus had been reached. More than a little put out, the salesman suggested a reasonable price and was grudgingly told OK. He could finally call his customer back. When he did call back, he found out that they had bought the same material from someone else, for less money, and it had already been delivered.

If the committee is formal, things will go very differently. They are extremely conscientious of the value of their own time. After all, they are highly paid, valuable managers, so they stack up several requests for expenditures and hold a meeting. I use the term "meeting" loosely. Bickering, petty objections, and political infighting often takes up much of the time. What seemed like a simple discussion can drag on for hours. Often things are rejected at this point even if there is no logical reason for the rejection. If the request is approved, however, all those on the committee are safe. Should the requested work not produce the expected results, no one can point a finger at any one person and blame them. Well, they can, but it won't do any good, because they spread the risk. If it does happen to produce the expected results, they'll all pat each other on the back, while secretly claiming all the credit themselves.

Take a moment to consider the costs of this. All the managers, from the one who sent the request through those who passed it on, have to have their rears covered, so they document everything. They say this is to decrease the possibility of distortion of original intent. These forms and requests have to go through the proper channels. There's a colossal waste of paper, or computer time, time, and, therefore, money. In large corporations, there will be dozens, perhaps hundreds of these requests going at any one time. You have to have the clerical staff to deal with all this processing, don't you? Every time the request went to, and through, a level it added to the clerical costs.

On top of those costs, are the costs of the committee itself. They often spend more money to talk about the request than the cost of the original request. Say they take up a boardroom for so many hours, have meals catered in, have to have their secretaries at the ready. How much money did the company waste because they've taught their employees not to make decisions, not to take any risks? That is not even taking into account the business that was probably lost or the hours of lowered productivity because of the length of time the request took to make the full loop. It's ironic, isn't it? They're spending all of this money trying to cling to the money that they have. And are wasting. It's not about profit at all. It's about "It's mine, don't touch it." Controlling money is the ultimate control mechanism.

This also doesn't include another "hidden" cost of these excessive layers. Have you ever heard the old saying "an idle mind is the devil's workshop"? If there are too many layers, managers won't have enough meaningful work to do. They'll use the excess time to goof off and hone their political skills. This is a huge morale killer. They also spend the time thinking up unrealistic rules and useless projects to saddle their lower levels with. Again, another huge morale killer. And a colossal waste of the employees' time. I know you've heard that time is money. You waste time, and you might as well be giving all of your product or service away for free for that period.

At each step in this process, the request was slowed down. It went through layers of management populated by NO men who know better than to take risks in the company. Even a committee can only make so many "mistakes" before it will disband or begin denying every request because it's just not worth the risk to them. It's all about staying safe and warm in their little boxes. They want to keep their job, their paycheck, and their status. All you'll get are excuses and reasons why things can't be done. There is every impediment to action. Why? Because action involves risk. Fear, though they won't give it that name, takes over. They don't want to lose what they have. The company making a profit is, all too often, lost or put at the bottom of the priority list. The gritty truth is that the objective becomes to allow one or a few at the top to control every aspect of the business and all the employees. But! They don't believe in micromanaging-just ask them…

They do not look at the people surrounding the request. The human element has been taken out entirely. That human element could have made them the cost of the request times 10, but they will never know that. Worst of all, they won't even consider it lost because they don't even realize that it could have been theirs. Nothing in these unnecessary layers is positive or oriented toward what should be the goal: taking care of the customers and the employees who care for them.

One thing that can be said about corporations, and agreed upon by everyone, is that they are complex organizations. Thing is, folks, they are far more complicated than they have to be. There is beauty and efficiency in simplicity.

Have no more layers than are absolutely necessary. This minimizes the number of potential places for a NO stamp to be placed on any worthwhile project and seriously cuts down on clerical costs. Not to mention that cleaning up your organization in this way is essential to it running smoothly and profitably.

Send authority and responsibility back down the chain of command to where it belongs. Yes, I said "where it belongs." Or, said another way (if it makes you feel better): give your managers authority to manage. That's what they're there for. That's what you pay them to do. Let them do it. Hold them to high standards, and, if they can't handle the job, move them out of management. A manager should be able to make any and all decisions for his department without worrying about what negative repercussions will come down from above.

Why should a high level manager be deciding if a company vehicle should be repaired and by what mechanic? Why should a high level manager be deciding how many pens a person should use each month? They shouldn't be making those decisions. They have no true conception of the results. Those decisions should be made by the appropriate lower or middle level manager. Upper levels of management should be focused on the forest, not the trees. That doesn't mean they're not aware of the individual trees, only that they are more focused on planning the care for the whole forest.

How about a couple of real life examples to fully illustrate this point?

A medical facility supervisor decided to ban any pharmaceutical company's pens from the clinics. The cost to the clinic was $4,000 a month they hadn't budgeted. With planning, the clinic could have adjusted, but the supervisor didn't speak to the clinic before issuing the "edict."

A salesman operated a service station associated with a well known oil company and was acquainted with some of their Field Production Managers. He asked one of them why it was that small, independent oil companies who bought old wells from the big company could make them profitable while the big company couldn't.

The manager explained that the big company had to fill out a form requesting authority to work on a well. The form had to be approved by a local field manager before it went to the corporate office where it went through several layers of management and scrutiny by engineering and accounting. Then, at a committee meeting, it was talked over. It would be returned, after about a year, usually marked "not economically feasible." So, the requested work wasn't approved, and, instead of getting the well producing again, they left it sitting until they decided to sell it or plug it.

At the small, independent company, however, over coffee in the morning, they would decide to pull it. They would, then, usually have a rig set up on it that afternoon to replace a worn out pump or a joint of tubing that had a hole in it, etc. They would fix the problem and move on, usually having it up and running again that afternoon or the next day. By making those simple changes, the new owner would commonly bring production back to its previous level or, more often, exceed the previous output.

A major oil company a few years ago sold an old well that was down to 2 barrels of oil per day production. The small, independent oil producer who bought it did a simple clean up and brought it back to more than 50 barrels of oil per day. It kept producing at that rate. The major company sent a memo to their engineering department to this effect: if anyone authorized the sale of a well and an independent producer was able to significantly improve its output, they would automatically be fired! Let your imagination try to digest that!

This can't-do is a far cry from the American can-do exhibited by the creation of the Panama Canal. When progress was slow, they went out and hired one of the best railroad construction men they could find. The new manager had done things people thought were impossible when building railroads in the northwest part of the United States in the late 1880s. If a job was "impossible," he did it. When he took over the Panama Canal project, he immediately sized up the problems, the scope of the project, and what type of people he needed. He found an army doctor who could control yellow fever if he had the resources. The doctor was given virtually a blank check and told to do it! Immediately, if not sooner. The whole canal project needed equipment. An order was immediately placed for 48 steam shovels, railroad engines, track, and on and on. The job was completed in good order, using lights they built to work 24/7, and within the projected time. Money wasn't wasted or misused and neither was time. "Can't" didn't exist.

In World War II, when supplies were being held up because there was a shortage of the proper forms, they wrote a receipt on anything they had on hand. They were going to get those damn materials where they were needed-and fast. When ships were in short supply to move equipment, they cut the trucks and jeeps into parts, loaded them onto aircraft, and welded them back together at the forward bases. Can you imagine what might have happened if they had waited for the proper authorization? Thankfully we don't have to. People who make history rarely let themselves get caught up in the drama that is bureaucracy.

Without risk, there can be no possibility of reward. If you want the reward of a stellar, profitable, solid business, you'll have to give honest thought about the risks I'm suggesting.

4: KISS

Inside the layers (which are, in themselves, impediments), there are more roadblocks to the efficiency of the company. The inner workings of each department get so twisted around that most of the logic is completely removed as those in management attempt to shove things, and people, into nice, neat little boxes. Too many layers of management takes away the personal touch. Many managers don't really interact with or know people below their level on a personal basis. Only abuses get discussed with the management team, and the mantra is that if one employee does this, others probably will too. If a complaint goes up the chain, it's easier to create more rules. Many of these rules are, all too often, stupid. The thing is, most upper level management assumes that their subordinates are dumb, lazy, that they can't be trusted with decisions, and that they will cheat, steal, and lie at every opportunity. (Few lower, and even middle, managers seem to realize that they fall within this group, that the man at the top, or small group at the top, consider themselves the only competent ones.)

How do they control the masses of little box people? The book, of course. Make sure everything is done by the book. They'll beat people with it if they have to. Make the employees fill out forms, or have conference calls, on every little thing. They want to know what is going on in their kingdom. For the things and times for which it's not appropriate to have forms or calls, make sure that there are enough rules in place so that the employees are in predictable places doing predictable things at predictable times.

Here is an irony. The corporation is always harping on communications. The reality is that it only runs one way. From the bottom up. Little to no information is communicated down. The people downstream are expected to do what they are told, no questions asked. Great environment for the rumor mill! The human species will speculate about anything that affects their lives if there is inadequate information. In all too many cases, management wouldn't like what the rumors were about. No problem. No one is going to include management in this informational loop anyway, so they are blissfully unaware.

If the employee has to fill out a form every time they have to go to supply for a box of pens, at least the boss will know who's a pen hog. They'll know that the office is using more pens than they should "need." They'll know who to confront about excessive pen usage. They'll have no idea that Bob is the only one who will take the time to fill out the form and that everyone will come grab the pens from him as soon as they're in his possession. The employee that gets in trouble will be the one who was actually following procedure. That doesn't make a whole lot of sense does it? And it surely doesn't induce any of the other employees to fill out those ridiculous forms.

Then there are the conference calls or call reports. Generally those who schedule conference calls do so with absolutely no regard to the actual business itself. As long as it fits into their schedule, so they'll be on time for tee time, they don't care if it pulls their managers away at the busiest time of day. Not to mention the call reports that salesmen are required to make at the end of the day. Is it more important for them to be on the phone blowing smoke so you won't fire them or out acutally getting the business that will bring in the revenue? It seems to be blowing smoke.

Yes, I'm reasonable, and I understand some forms may be necessary to run the business. That's a given. But! Keep them simple. Eliminate all of the eye clutter. Human tendency, programmed in us by society, is to complete forms entirely whether it is logical or not. Folks, all that extra writing obscures the important information. If your people actually fill out the forms (which they may not do because it feels like wasted time and effort), much of the information is irrelevant and will not be used. Everything is a cost factor. Over time, a lot of man hours are spent filling out extremely detailed forms and more are often spent going through those same forms at a later date, only to find out that the information is no longer relevant. Keep information requested on forms to the absolute minimum. Nuts and bolts only. Most forms that are too detailed were invented by new or incompetent people. They have a line for every contingency. You end up having to hunt for the lines where important information goes. Rather than this rubbish, use "KISS". Anything extra that might be desirable can be put on a blank area labeled "Notes" or on an attached add-on sheet.

Just for grins, I recently tried to reduce part of the job I do to a checklist. After three pages it was apparent it was a fool's errand. No list exists for every possible contingency because problems come up that didn't exist in the past.

The more information that is compiled, the more it may seem necessary to hire someone to be "in charge" of it. The more inefficiency, the more employees needed. Evaluate your needs. Are the forms absolutely necessary? Keeping extra information because you *might* need it can get expensive. When handling the industrial sales for a former employer, my secretary/clerk and I operated a company within a company. We kept paperwork to a minimum. A couple of times a year, we would sit down and review what we were doing and why. We would look at some of the records we kept and figure out if, through the course of the year, we put too many hours into it. If we did actually need that information, we could dig it out of our files in a couple of hours. As an example: we started out keeping a running record of how many pounds of aluminum were sold to each account through the year. No one ever asked for those numbers, and they served no useful purpose. If we had ever needed it, we could take it off our scheduling sheets. The sales figures we obtained from accounting were adequate for our purposes, so we stopped keeping a running record of it. No brainer there.

Keep no records that are not economically important or logically required. If you decide that a form is necessary, make sure your workers know that forms are secondary to getting their job done. Paperwork waits; customers, suppliers, and all types of people don't. Certain records are essential. Those you do, of course, but keep it simple. All too many of the records kept in the big corporations are for one purpose only. Covering someone's a** in case something goes wrong.

Call reports and conference calls also fit into this category. Is it absolutely necessary? Or, in being honest with yourself, do you see that it's just another form of micromanagement? Huge amounts of money are wasted on micromanaging. Not just in the dollars themselves but the time it takes up that could equal dollars. Try this: If you have a conference call for all your salesmen, calculate the value of their time. Don't use salaries. Divide the annual work hours of the individual into the gross dollars of their sales. Take that number for each person and total them. That's going to be a significant value for an hour. Yes, you have to keep in contact with your people. Communication is essential to a profitable business. There is a difference, however, between a group discussion focused on getting down to the real information about what is going on and a weekly conference call filled with "we're planning on…" "we might be able…" etc. If a call is necessary, be mindful of the timing. You don't want to interfere with the attendees' ability to deliver the results you are asking for by having them on these calls while their customers or suppliers are most available or most likely to need their attention.

Another huge waste of resources is the time spent by all people of responsibility in the corporation doing CYA. Keep records of everything, e-mails, text messages, inquiries, recommendations, anything that might possibly be used against you if you didn't have documentation to prove your innocence. There are those in most big companies that will gladly throw you under the bus. You can protect yourself somewhat by arranging for the company to only buy low rider buses. (Oh, but only the top man has the authority to make that decision.)

When evaluating these parts of your business, watch out for those who retain a sense of power by controlling information. They are an impediment. All pertinent information must be readily available to those who need it. Look hard at what needs to be restricted and what doesn't. If it does need to be restricted, it does. If it doesn't, make sure your people know where to get it. Simple as that.

Now let's talk about those heaps of rules. It doesn't occur to the top people, or perhaps they simply don't care, that the rigid, often petty, and oppressive rules are actually a hinderance to creating a dynamic and fully productive workplace. They have a cumulative effect, creating an extremely stressful working environment, especially for good employees who will constantly wonder if they are going to break one rule or another, either by accident or in the pursuit of doing their job to the best of their ability. No matter what level the employee is on, not only will he still be in a box, albeit a different one depending on the job, he will still be mired in those inflexible rules.

Say a very important customer needs three pieces of a manufactured item for trials on a new application. They only come in lots of 100. The last guy who deviated from this was fired. This employee is faced with a choice: follow company policy, tell the customer no, risk losing them, and, therefore, his job as a result, or go against company policy, get the items, retain the customer, and risk losing his job if he gets caught. Either way, he is at risk.

This might seem unrealistic to you. Surely this doesn't really happen. A true example: One job I had, I started as a janitor in a production machine shop. The work wasn't hard, and there was a bit of spare time. Not being comfortable doing nothing, I would find something useful to do when I'd finished my duties. Under the machines there were metal shavings, dirt, and trash that had been there for years. I decided to clean up. I had cleaned out under several machines and was working on another when the maintenance manger came by. And stopped me. He told me not to do that. He said my job was to keep the metal shavings bins empty, sweep the aisles, and keep the restrooms clean and no more… He'd rather have me sit on the clock doing nothing after my duties were completed than step outside my box and take initiative. Follow the rules. Do no more, no less. Stay in your box.

Big corporations, with few exceptions, are oppressive places to work because of their stacks of rules. When setting rules or guidelines, look at all sides of the issue and weigh all aspects. Is the rule necessary? How is it likely to be received? Was this a reaction to one person's screw up? Is someone abusing a privilege? How often does the problem occur? Is it because of government rules? OSHA? EPA? DOT? etc.

All too often, petty rules are issued because someone in management didn't have the courage to call an employee in for counseling when they were abusing a privilege. It's easier to send out a blanket rule. The problem with this is that the ones who pay attention are your good employees, and they don't need more pressure. The person who caused a new law to be issued, more than likely, doesn't care.

It also needs to be taken into account what will happen when the rule is broken. For example: Anyone parking in the executive's parking spots will be terminated. If your top salesman breaks the rule, in a hurry on his way to a meeting, will he be fired? Would someone who doesn't produce as much? What if they are breaking it for the good of the company, to save a customer or account? What will this difference in treatment do to morale? Is that really worth it to you?

Rules have a cumulative effect. You don't want your employees to start their day wondering if they have violated a rule unknowingly, if they will be able to help their customers today or if a decision hasn't been reached yet about whatever it was they needed. This takes a toll on your workforce. This "low level" anxiety can cause a host of health issues, even in young people, causing more sick days, and it interferes with their productivity. If they're scared of breaking rules or stepping on someone's toes, they are not going to be able to perform their job to their full potential. At best. At worst, they are going to completely shut down and perform the absolute minimum to get by and still get paid.

If your workers are doing the minimum to get by, you are going to have to hire more of them to do the work. An oppressive and unresponsive company is going to be an unprofitable one. Outside death and taxes, the only guarantee is change. Nothing stays the same forever. If you try to hang on to outdated and petty rules, you will be reducing the profitability of your company in subtle ways. Yes, a certain amount of order is required for a large organization to function properly. Just make sure you design a bypass for most functions in case of emergency. Believe me, there will be one sooner or later. Probably sooner.

Avoid cut and dried rules and edicts. Issue company based guidelines only if necessary. And make the managers do their jobs. It's their job to manage the people under them. They don't need HR to issue more rules so they can have a cop out of actually getting their hands dirty. They need to know what needs to get done, and they need to make sure that it does. That said, it will be much easier for the manager to do their job effectively if they aren't, every moment of their day, wracking their brains trying to remember rule number 1671 so they can attempt to enforce it. The Roman Kato said, nearly 2000 years ago, and it's still applicable today, "We used to suffer from crime; now we suffer from laws." Company rules are laws within the company. Keep that in mind when you look over your company policy book. If it is necessary for the profitability of the company, keep it. If not, it's time to stretch yourself a little and toss it. A good rule of thumb: don't have policies that are subjective, that are actually unlikely to be applied to everyone, and that are difficult to enforce.

I'd like to end this chapter with a story from history. On December 7th of 1941, during the attack on Pearl Harbor, a marine didn't have time to go get the key to an ammunitions locker holding machine gun ammunition. Doing the most natural thing in the world, at that particular moment in time, he smashed the lock and grabbed what they needed.

Afterward his lieutenant filed court martial papers on him for destroying government property. The lock that was damaged. From our objective vantage point, we know that's ridiculous. The lieutenant, though, was just following the rules. Unfortunately, there are all too many "managers" in the corporate world that are no more intelligent than the above mentioned lieutenant.

Paperwork, time wasted, rigidity in the execution of the rules. I'm sure there were better ways to spend their time in the stressful days following that incident. This example might seem a little extreme in comparison to what we've been talking about here. It's only that way because of objectivity. Look at your many layers of management, forms and communications, your rules with an objective eye. You might find things that will surprise you and, hopefully, make you think.

(And just in case you were wondering, a superior officer told the lieutenant that no charges would be filed against the marine.)

5: To Spend or Not to Spend When Money is Tight

Box people are very easy to control. The reason? They do what they're told. That's a good thing, right? Not really. Now, hold on to your hat a minute, and let me finish. The problem is that they usually end up doing just what they're told. And no more. They do the absolute minimum from clock-in to clock-out. This may not seem like too bad a thing. It seems like a fact of business.

It always becomes an issue, folks. People in the upper layers of management just don't think that it could possibly be linked to cash flow problems when they begin to spring up. Instead of going to the actual root of the problem, they react in very predictable ways. When money is tight, the top people are going to start looking for ways to reduce costs. (All the while pointing fingers at everyone else, because, after all, they were each doing their job and making sure their underlings were too.)

Now that the company is seeing a steady decrease of profit, they start to get a little panicky. It's human nature; it happens. Instead of stepping back and objectively looking at the issues, all of them, the usual reaction is one of fear. They begin making excuses to hoard money and seriously cut expenses. They've shifted into a negative mode of thinking. At this point, they will not even consider money spent on reasonable risk for potential growth. (This oftentimes includes research and development, because it is too unpredictable. This is very detrimental to the company.) Then the company will turn to its accounting department for all the answers. This turns out to be a mistake.

Numbers do fit nicely into boxes. Way better than people do, by the way. There is an inherent problem with this, though. It is easy for them to say, "Let's cut this expense over here or that one over there." Numbers, unlike people, will not complain when this is done. Those in charge will move them about, do some subtraction, take out a couple things, and the numbers won't say a word. The thing is: those number actually do represent things, even people sometimes. This isn't a math problem in your third grade classroom. There's a lot more at stake here. People in charge of stuffing the numbers into the preferred range often forget this. Every single one of those numbers that is changed impacts people, quality of items or service, and, so, the business itself. In the end, those in charge of the numbers might be able to save the company a couple hundred thousand dollars a year by cutting in a few areas. But at what cost?

A true example of this. A business was taken over by investment brokers, and they were stuck with their purchase because no one else wanted it. They called in professional accounting people. Their recommendation? Cut inventory. If an item hadn't sold X number of units in the previous year, scrap it. One product, they only sold 6 units a years, so they got rid of it. While most of the business lost was smaller accounts, this one particular product had a multimillion dollar account hinged on it. They had to turn around and begin to produce it again.

A new hardware store moved into town a while ago now, part of a corporate chain. It was an okay place to shop. Average quality items with attractive pricing. They did well for a couple of years. Then, one day I went to their store to buy some fasteners. They were out of stock of that item and a few others. It happens, so I didn't think anything about it at the time. I went back again a while later. This time there were more empty shelves, and they didn't even have half of what I needed. I tried one more time a while later. It was worse. A few months after that, I saw a going-out-of-business sign. Their idea of a going-out-of-business sale was a 10% price reduction. This cut in inventory drove this business into the ground (among other things I'm sure, but this was a major contributor). There was no way they could compete in a marketplace when five other companies in their community had the same offerings at competitive prices and kept them stocked. They couldn't sell what they didn't have.

A group of us were having a morning problem-solving session over coffee at work one day. We were a bunch of workaholics trading information and finding solutions. Our accountant came in, and we were discussing inventory with her. I got a bit exasperated and remarked that all accountants hate inventory. She immediately denied the assertion. Then she followed it up with, "Ideally, though, you have everything drop shipped to your customers and don't have inventory." I rest my case.

The scramble to cut costs by any means necessary has a detrimental impact on the company. Whether those cuts are in inventory, in quality of wholesaler, in the number of scratch pads and pens the company provides, or in the people who make the business run matters not. It leads to an inevitable decline in quality of service and goods, and that leads to a smaller loyal customer base. The stress of being unable to do their job will cause higher employee turnover. Though the company saved hundreds of thousands of dollars, they now have to deal with the "hidden" economic ramifications of that. They will, usually, cut more costs. This cycle will continue ad infinitum while the company slowly bleeds out.

The problem is that the entire orientation of the corporate model is to put all effort into not making mistakes. Expanding sales, developing market, etc. get lip service only. Why is that? Because those things cost money and attempting to do them is a risk with said money. Those in charge of the money are so afraid to lose some of it that they won't risk spending it. They'd rather keep what they have. They begin to focus on small, petty, or insignificant things that make one appear to have the company's best interest in mind, ie cutting down on the number of ballpoint pens used every year. It's the safe thing to do. Folks, if saving pennies by buying fewer scratch pads or pens is where the business is, it's already going under, and you just don't know it yet.

You don't make money by saving money. You make money by spending it wisely. Can you think of a successful company of any size that saved their way to success? Cutting costs is not the answer to putting money on the bottom line. That's a very negative approach. This is a tough one, because fear will kick in when profit dips closer to the red, so, often, cutting costs is the first instinctive reaction. Key word here: reaction. Fear is making the decision for you.

Remember the first thing you should do in a panic is: don't panic. Get emotions out of the picture and make a realistic assessment. First how can you turn the negatives into positives? What creative solutions can you come up with to turn this around?

Think positive. Is it really necessary to cut prices? Don't think cheap here, think value. Maintain your margin and price as much as possible. Instead help your prospect reduce his overall operating costs by applying your company's products and experience. Go on a hard market push, and go find companies to help. Not with the attitude of trying to sell but in adding value. Perhaps your employees can be taught to add value to your products by showing customers more care than they would get anywhere else. (Hold up, though, you don't get that by pushing your employees. We'll get to that later.)

What parts of the budget are absolutely necessary? One place that often gets its budget cut first is Research and Development. This is very shortsighted. Change is inevitable. Nothing stays the same forever. All products will age if R&D are not kept up. With no improvement on products or no new products, the company will die. If you are trying to save money now so that you can go back to putting money into R&D, that's a dream. Something will always come up if you're in "cost saving" mode. Your research and development will steadily decline until it no longer exists. Then the same will happen to your company. The leading abrasives company for years was National Carborundum. They stopped developing newer products and were eventually absorbed by a new dynamic competitor named Norton Abrasives. I was selling industrial supplies at one point, and abrasives were a very active line for us. This included grinding stones of all types from those used to clean up wells to the big wheels used in the manufacturing processes. The Norton company fielded very well trained technical representatives. I learned a great deal from them in small, informal training sessions. They were also as close as a phone call if a question needed an answer. Because of this, I always felt comfortable selling their products. Their products were superior because of this R&D. Companies like DuPont and 3M have put sizable resources into R&D, and they have survived over the long run. If they can do it, so can you. You just have to keep assessing where the money is going.

Are there any unnecessary projects going on? Put them on hold, if at all possible, until times get better. All too often corporations will lay off workers but the office renovation for the top dogs goes right on. Somehow it is a lot easier to get approval on capital expenditures amounting to hundreds of thousands of dollars than it is to get approval for a box of pens once a month. The big spend usually involves the top managers. They'll draw up plans, justify costs, obtain bids, lay it all out in a detailed proposal that is impressive to look at. It will be approved. Down on the front lines, though, because there aren't enough pens to go around, your workers are struggling to write out their reports because their pens keep getting commandeered by others. Assess everything objectively, no sacred cows. Put large projects on temporary hold. Every cut can have long term consequences. Do what you must, but think positive. Even a cut back may have pluses.

Is regular maintenance getting done, tools being replaced as needed, or are those things on hold because of cost cutting? Old computers need to be replaced every few years. If not, all data processing will take longer than necessary which means more people on the payroll. Things like this are significantly more important than getting the CEO's office renovation done on time or the top executive going ahead with their five day fling in Jamaica. A worn out tool can make a job take twice the time to accomplish. The company is paying someone for that time. That's not even considering someone being injured because of a damaged tool. As I said, if saving money in these little petty areas is critical to keeping the corporation afloat, then bankruptcy is not too far behind. Don't get trapped into using the cheapest source for commodity items, either. Use an optimum source. Optimum is a word few people in the corporate world have heard and even fewer understand. A rough layman's definition as it applies to goods and services is the best source for the price. Note that it's not always the cheapest.

Are you thinking about switching service companies for one reason or another? Take time to fully consider. Even in large cities, for example, there may not be one good vehicle repair shop. If there are more than five good heat and air service companies in a metroplex, you are lucky. The rest will help relieve you of your money, but you will get poor value for the amount of money you spent.

Say you need a good mechanic's shop to keep your vehicles going. Choices? How about dealerships? They will fix your vehicles; but it's going to cost you big time- in time and money spent. Put a truck in a dealer's shop, and you'll be lucky to get it back in less than a week. While you wait, you can pay other employees overtime to pick up the slack or rent a vehicle. National service chains are not much better or any cheaper.

Find an independent shop that does good work at a fair price and develop a working relationship with them. If you team with them instead of constantly trying to get them to be cheaper, they'll take care of you. You get them down too cheap, you might put them out of business. (But, hey, you can always go back to the dealership, right?) Not all shops are honest or responsive. It may take trying several to find an optimum shop. Rewards. You can often get one day turn around. If your truck is operable, and you know the problem, your mechanic can have the parts on hand before you drop off the truck. Work with them, and they'll tell you how to prevent problems at no charge. They will check your vehicles thoroughly and warn you of needed work. For petty things, they won't even bill you.

When it comes to service companies, always remember that the good ones are even more scarce than good workers. Find the right one and stick with them as long as they take care of you. A good working relationship with your service company can save you many a headache and a lot of dollars.

Do you really need to make cuts in the workforce, or is there another alternative? Consider more innovative ways to weather a tough market. Reduce manager's salaries by a set amount or percentage across the board. Most should be able to stand a few months of that. Hourly people all too often live from pay check to pay check and would suffer accordingly if they are cut. An innovative way one employer skipped a layoff of hourly employees was to offer unpaid time off for negotiable lengths of time. Each employee told their department head they would like to take off a few days, weeks, or even months. More than two-thirds of the employees had worked there for more than 10 years, and some for more than 30 years. Their children were grown, and they had some money but lacked time to take extended vacations or do projects. They saved enough man hours that they didn't have to lay off any of the sixty people that would have been required.

More often than not, corporations will cut at the field level first where it will cost them the most. If all else fails and cuts have to be made, start in the office. The people most directly connected to bringing in the money are in the field. Depending on the industry, field tech training can take anywhere from one to several years before the tech can operate completely on their own. Even delivery people can require several weeks of on-the-job training if simple mechanical installations are part of their job. Let's say a green delivery person hooks up a chemical pump wrong. A dog comes along and licks spilled chemicals because they taste good. The result: a dead dog. Many dogs have died this way because mechanics left a pan of automotive anti-freeze on the floor. Costly! Whether it was a mutt who was a family pet or a prize animal who was worth thousands of dollars and had a blood line all the way back to King Arthur's time. That's just a simple example of what can happen with making too many cuts at field level. Do just the opposite of the corporate practice. *It's a lot easier to find clerical help than it is to find experienced field technicians.*

Want to cause a really big fuss when doing a layoff? Do the unthinkable. Lay off excess managers! Most middle managers in corporations are generalists. They have only a superficial knowledge of what's going on. Most grasp concepts quickly, but they don't slow their minds up enough to learn the details that are necessary to fully understand and perform the work.

Crazy? The large manufacturing company I worked for for years was taken over by a group of salesmen. Not one of them was capable of going out into the plant and performing anything but the simplest jobs. Middle managers in most corporations are similar. Keep your skilled workers if at all possible. They can be hard or impossible to replace when times get better. Truth is: generalist middle managers are really only worth a dime a dozen. Harsh? Take anyone with half a brain, give them a title, and put them in an office. They need to do only what they are specifically told to do and nothing else. They are not allowed to make any decisions. Those are left to the genius of the top managers. The primary skills of all too many managers are those that are involved in making people above them feel important. So in a layoff situation, check the value of an employee and then act accordingly.

I am aware that one of the major sources of expenditures for a company is the people they employ. This is, however, another place that it is shortsighted to cut costs. The cost/benefit for each member of your team should be evaluated. That said, if you want good people, you have to pay for them. If you don't, you could end up training them for your competition who will pay better. A true example: There was a running joke at Adult

Beverages that Soft Drinks was their "training grounds." Soft Drinks treated their employees so badly that, when it was possible, the employees would leave and start working at Adult Beverages already understanding the job to be done. Adult Beverages didn't have to pay for any training because Soft Drinks did it for them. And Soft Drinks instilled a respect for Adult Beverages in them, because they knew how much better they were being treated. They worked harder for Adult Beverages because they actually took care of them.

A friend of mine who was leaving Soft Drinks sent a letter to the regional manager outlining the short comings of their management policies and even went as far as to assign dollar value to the high turnover. He then recommended the changes that would solve the problem and put a lot more money on the bottom line. I told him it would promptly get filed in the trash cans and any copies hunted down and disposed of. He never heard from them. Probably best, though, since Adult Beverages likes the present arrangement.

Workers who are positive thinkers and plugged into reality are rare finds that will pay huge dividends if properly managed. Whether you're talking about accountants, engineers, clerical staff, managers, mechanics, salesmen, cooks, or janitors, exceptional workers are the exception, not the rule.

Often companies are so busy pointing fingers, and taking that extra few boxes of pens off the budget, that they completely overlook the much larger wastes of money. Unproductive and deadweight employees being one. If you are going to cut somewhere, start there. But! Make sure you've honestly and objectively evaluated them so that you know exactly which ones are deadweight and which ones have a bad rap from jealous coworkers.

Wasting productive employee's time on trivialities is completely useless, which we've already talked about briefly. Excessive forms, useless surveys, and the like take time out of their day which could be used doing something that contributes to the bottom line. In addition to this, has it ever occurred to anyone that the employees might actually want to take a survey (quickly, efficiently, and perhaps even on their own time) if the company was treating them right and the survey would produce useful information.

This brings us to a very important point. Put responsibility back on the managers to manage. Give them a budget or agree on one. Everything in that manager's charge is decided by him/her. They are expected to file a report on the total expenditures each month for the previous month. If they go over, an explanation would be attached. They should be allowed some flexibility even here (say no prior approval if it's less than 20% over). Large projects and costs obviously need coordination because of cash flow, market changes, etc.

At the end of a fiscal year, a manager should have a detailed complete record of all expenditures. Upper management can make a detailed review if they choose. If not, it goes on file for future reference. If the manager doesn't use all of his budget, and it didn't "cost" the company, he should be congratulated. If he spent more money and increased profitability by doing it, he would be acknowledged.

This removal of the need for upper management micromanaging at a base level frees up a manager and his team to get it done. For example: the office needs computer paper. Someone used more than a normal amount due to several large bids that all hit at the same time. In a rush, no one thought to order more paper. Options: order through the most "economical source," which entails getting a purchase order approved by three levels of management and taking a week to get it ok'd or let an hourly employee go to a nearby office supply store and buy enough to get by. Allowing the manager and those under him to make these decisions instills initiative and a get-it-done attitude, which will pay huge dividends over time.

This calls for courage. Loosening that death grip on the need for control. Control should come from the immediate supervisor. He is the one responsible. If a supervisor has someone under him that he can't trust to make such decisions, he doesn't allow them the chance to do so or he gets rid of them (unless they have some offsetting redeeming qualities). Upper management has no need to know immediately that you ran out of paper. If upper management has time to get involved in such trivia, they aren't needed.

All of this takes arm's length objectivity. You have to formulate flexible, long-range goals, and you have to be ready and willing to adapt. The question is not whether to save or spend money. The question is how to save or spend money wisely and objectively. It's not easy, but it is worth it. Like anything worth doing, it's worth putting the effort into. It's more than worth doing well.

6: Sales

I worked in sales for a number of years, and, not being much of a talker, I spent a lot of time listening and observing. One disturbing trend I observed was the lack of quality training. Most of it is corporate oriented propaganda with a smattering of sales thrown in. How does the company expect their salesmen to succeed without realistic training? It's unfair and illogical. Sales managers usually copy the corporate model and do things the same way as their competitors. If you want to win, you would do well to consider not copying your competition. Do you really want to be another "me too"?

There is a myth in the corporate world that you can force sales by aggressively attacking the market and pressuring your salesmen to increase sales immediately. Perhaps this is a good strategy in some markets, but, in my experience, it is a very poor one in most. All their emphasis is on the sale. They try to push their products or services out into the market, worrying only about monthly or quarterly sales. They do whatever it takes to look good right now, to push some numbers up in the short term. They completely disregard the long term.

Large accounts are almost always the objective. Trading in millions of dollars is good, right? They push for volume. What happens? The company ends up subsidizing "junk business." Why is it called junk business? The account is going to produce a lot of sales dollars, our salesman was the guy who got the sale. What's not to love?

Junk accounts have little or no loyalty. They will hammer you down on price to the last penny. They are never satisfied, call often to complain about every little thing, and make nearly impossible demands. They take up technical department and shipping and delivery time. They are slow to pay, and they often refuse to work with you when problems come up. If materials, for some reason, don't meet normal specifications but could be used elsewhere by the customer, you work with them, sometimes giving discounts or delayed billings. Both parties benefit. However, difficult accounts won't do that. They tell you to get it out of there and replace it immediately with the right material, and they don't care what you do with the off-spec material. These junk accounts will seldom follow recommendations and complain about the results in any case. They're lawsuit prone to boot. The objective of profit has been obscured, if not lost entirely. At this point, it's about prestige, who has that big account. Most companies continually go after accounts such as these, attempting to service them into cooperation. That's an impossible feat. Let your competition have these. It will keep them busy and out of your hair.

The actual net profit on large, junk accounts is sometimes less than zero. Yes, you can be paying them to buy from you. Gross profit all too often is less than 10%. But hey, it's a $5M account based on annual purchases. Contrast that with a good account that brought $1M, but you netted 25-30%. I want a $1M at 25% any day over less than 10%. A big fudge factor comes into play. Ten percent of $5M is $500,000, while 25% of $1M is $250,000. What sales often won't mention is added work that gets lost in the overhead numbers or the occasional $200,000-$300,000 in returned merchandise that the buyer decided they didn't want. In some cases, the customer demanded special products tailored for their use only. They decided they didn't want it, and you get to pick it up and issue a credit. You have no other market for it, and you have to pay to dispose of it. It doesn't get mentioned in the sales department's annual total sales.

I have watched accounts like these for years. In one case, a major competitor bid a price of business so cheap they couldn't even break even. In another case, a competitor picked up a large junk account. Technical demands from the account were excessively costly. Margin was so tight that salesmen had to get prior approval just to buy someone's lunch at that account. On top of this, the account usually paid 5-6 months after each billing. The company trying to service this account had a dozen people dedicated to that single customer. In another case, we had a problem account. A new competitor in our market took the business from us then let the customer get stretched out on paying their bills. The result: 6 months later, that account filed for bankruptcy, and the competitor got burned for $60,000.

Folks, you don't want all the business; you want all the good business.

There is a fallacy that the best salesman is the one with the most sales. This puts a lot of pressure on salespeople. They are always looking, sometimes desperately, for that next big account. What does that do to business? In most companies, each salesperson knows, even if only subconsciously, that they are in competition with all the other salespeople. If there is going to be a cutback, they don't want to get chopped. Because of this, the senior salesmen do no want to mentor or assist newer people. It's dangerous. That person could surpass them. They'll help if they're specifically told to do so, but only minimally.

Consider, though. You have several salesmen who consistently generate enough business to cover their salaries and make the company good money. They have long-term, loyal customers with good margin. In some markets, you can't go wrong if you have a hundred of them or more. Take all you can get. Any one of them may never make top salesman, but the group forms a solid business base that can often see you through business down times.

In the corporate model, the top salesman is the one with the most dollar volume at the end of the year. Profit margins all too often get left out of the rankings system. Remember, you can't stay in business just trading dollars.

Salespeople are, often, so busy with politics, that, when a current customer or account calls, they are hesitant to answer. It costs them valuable time to listen to the problem. This inattention drives business to competitors. You get a call from a prospect that their current supplier won't return their calls. They're probably out trying to make their next big sale. They probably don't think they're going to make any more money from this, so they don't want to take the time to help. The customer has become an inconvenience. Little thought or effort goes into maintaining the relationship with the customer. After all, they already have his business. The salesman sees no immediate benefit from "going out of his way" to help. Even if he does grudgingly go out to help his customer, he will be extremely hesitant to ask for help himself should he need it to take care of the request. That's an admission of imperfection, and that could be a job killer in the corporate world.

Another factor here is technical assistance to back up the salesmen. It occurs all too often that samples sent in to labs will take from several days to several weeks before being analyzed and the information sent back out to the salesman. In the corporate model, compartmentalization is the rule. Laboratories often schedule work not with the market in mind but rather what's most convenient to the lab. No exceptions. Everything follows a set procedure. A little reality here. If the backlog of lab work is too great, they simply throw away any work over 30 days old and plead ignorance if someone asks about it. The salesman has no information for his customer, so he doesn't return calls and, possibly, loses the account.

I'm still waiting on some test results for samples sent to one of our suppliers over ten years ago. We were not a big account for them at that time.

What we're driving at here is that, in the corporate model, customers are inconvenient.

The typical corporate marketing strategy Sell, Sell, Sell is followed. It is a breeding ground for poor salespeople, who have little interest in the customer themselves. They've gained a lot of junk business, probably tried to expand their territory by getting someone else's added to theirs, pushed more product on customers than they actually needed or wanted, forgotten (at least a time or two) about a promise they made to a customer and had to rush around at the last minute when they finally remembered. And completely alienated their customer. Most likely they were applauded for a job well done.

In addition to all of this, after a salesman is "trained," it is generally implied to him, if not outright said, that he has a certain amount of time to make a certain target number in sales or his job is in jeopardy. This can create a deep, perhaps subconscious, desperation in the salesman. He has to sell, or he can't feed his family. We'll forget for a moment that most people can sense desperation and insecurity in a salesperson. After all, the prospects have been dealing with peddlers for years. When a salesman is not truly knowledgable about what they are selling, their only alternative is to jump right into their 'canned speech' presentation. When this happens, the salesman needs to be observant of the prospect's reaction. If the prospect starts to snore, it's ok to get up and leave.

To illustrate how well the peddler type salesman is viewed by a prospect, I'm going to tell a story from one of our salesmen. The average buyer in our market is normally approached by as many as 25 peddlers a year. They know the instant they see them that they want to sell them something. Our salesman made a cold call on a prospect. He entered the office and introduced himself and gave the prospect his calling card. The man looked at it, dropped it in the trash can, and said, "If you go out this side door, you can get back to your car faster."

We did eventually pick up that account. It came because another of our salespeople was selling to a service company who in turned contracted with them. A year after we started selling to them, the engineer who had been so curt called our other salesman and asked him to come by his office. They visited for over an hour and never discussed business. The engineer simply wanted to know who the person was that gave him good service.

People aren't interested in your needs or your company's needs. They are interested in their needs and who and what can best meet them.

At the end of the day, the salesman has to make his daily call report. As I said before, these are completely worthless. At best, they're a complete waste of time for those who do them. At worst, they make liars out of your salespeople. They have negligible sales results. They are, however, from the typical corporate playbook. You know that same book that everyone else is using, doing the exact same thing to their salespeople and their customers, causing business to dip closer and closer to that red ink over time. It's also a way to keep people in their little boxes.

In order to generate sales of your product or service, you have to, first, know and understand your market. What is your market, or potential market, macro and micro? What are your strengths and weaknesses vs. your competition's strengths and weaknesses. What is your market plan? What image do you want to project? Do you want to sneak in by word of mouth, or do you want to project an aggressive image? Do you want a combination of both? How do you want your customers to see you in a few years? How do you want your competitors to react when you show up on a survey they're on or you visit one of their accounts? What are your objectives, and how do you plan to achieve them?

Market research is essential. Analyze target areas and evaluate their potential. The marketing research doesn't always have to be done formally. A field salesman can often tell you every account and prospect in his area and even who the buying influences are. He can also tell you when there is no chance you will do business with certain prospects because your competition has it and is doing his job. Unfortunately he can also tell you who you won't be able sell to because your company made a mistake with them years before. If you ask, often you'll find he has long range plans of how he can pick up more business when a prospect sells, a manager retires, or he'll be first in line if a good competitor retires.

Do your homework on your competition. I'm not saying copy the way your competition does things, not at all. Please don't, in fact. Just know what they're doing and what the result is. Then you can exploit their weaknesses.

Emphasize long range business and market development. You might miss a couple of sales because of this in the beginning, but it will pay off in the long run. Don't allow fear to make you aggressively attack because you don't want to miss a sale or are afraid if you don't get this one it's going to lead to your inevitable failure. Fact is, you don't want all the business in a market. You only want the profitable business. No, it's not the same thing, as I've said.

I worked in sales over a dozen years, and I saw many different variations of market strategy and sales. It seems to me that corporations have always seen this as an inconvenience. They have to have money coming in, but developing a realistic, creative market strategy seems to be too much trouble, so they fall back on the corporate playbook. In reality it's always better, and less expensive, to create account loyalty than to always be dependent on new business.

The 80/20 rule fits most companies in many areas. It is true in this one as well. In this case, the rule states that 80% of your sales are generated by 20% of your salesmen. A typical corporate response to this is to start pressuring and micromanaging the other 80% of their salespeople and force them to sell more, try to make the world conform to what they want. Using call reports, etc., they reduce selling to a system that you could put on paper with numbers. I've watched this game played out by several large corporations. It never works.

Well, then, you might wonder, what does work? It's simple. In every aspect of every business type, it's good business to help people with their business, what they need and want. Orient your sales people to work with the customer. The prospective customer doesn't care about your need to make a sale to pay a bill or your workforce. He cares about what's in it for him. It's his money, and he'll spend it where he feels comfortable spending it.

Helping customers solve problems makes you better, and it helps them stay in business. In addition, it helps build a personal relationship that the competition often has no chance to break. What you learn on a one unit a year account may be the very thing you need on a big account years later. Small accounts will work with you better, especially on a problem that doesn't have an obvious cause or solution. Corrosion is a common problem encountered in oil and gas production. This causes failures in the down hole production equipment. We had a small customer that was putting chemical down a well to prevent metal loss, and they were still having problems. We worked with them and discovered the problem was the way they applied the treatments. That knowledge has been used many times over the years and has helped us avoid this happening again. Helping customers is always the golden rule. This is true in every business. Whether you're going the extra mile to help a customer pick out just the right shirt or trying to make things right when a guest in your restaurant didn't have a meal turn out right. Each of these things positively impacts the bottom line in subtle ways.

Train your salespeople to inquire about any problems or needs the prospect might have. If the prospect expresses that they are satisfied with their current supplier, compliment them on being fortunate. Then see if they will give you the names of the competitor's salesmen. Most companies have some good people. If the same name comes up again, try to contact that salesman and buy him lunch or a cup of coffee and get acquainted. You also may want him on your team some time in the future; however, you never want to start a feud with your competition. It's more beneficial to be seen as a competitor that plays fair. Be careful not to give away your marketing information, though.

If the competitor retires, you want to be next on the prospect's list. Drop by and visit a few minutes once a year. Don't try to sell them anything, you won't be welcome to come back again. If that salesman re-tires, you'll normally know it within a few days. Pay the prospect a timely visit. Don't go in there thinking about how much you're going to sell or how much you need to sell. Go in there with a "how can I help" attitude. Working with the prospect creates a relationship. You may not get a sale right away, but you are in it for the long haul. Oftentimes, what sold today was actually "sold" months ago.

Any over focus on monthly sales is usually time poorly spent. Quarterly sales are worth more attention, but 6 month and 12 month periods tell the real story. Salesmen usually have no immediate control over sales. Putting pressure on them simply stresses them out but to no gain. Sales today are often the result of events months or years earlier.

The thing is, in most markets, your competitors have access to or can provide the same products and services you do. Having a company philos-ophy of "take care of the customer" will last over the long haul where the competition will greatly suffer at times and some will go out of business. Take care of the customer, and the sales will take care of themselves. That might sound a little simplistic, and perhaps unrealistic. That's what your competitors are thinking, and that's why they're doing it the other way. They are thinking only about the sales, not about how they can help, how they can earn the business. It might be working out for them. Right now. In the long run, it's a great way to annoy and alienate people.

One of our top salesmen told me that if you picked up a new account and lost it in 30 days, you never had it to start with. To have an account, you have to develop a relationship.

People talk. Word of mouth is a great sales technique. So is devel-oping leads and helping your customers make money. The more money they make, the more money they can spend. There is no marketing effort required in this. You take care of what you have, and it grows.

Look at your top salesmen to figure out why they're at the top. It's very likely that you won't be able to get your 80% to produce as well as the 20%, but you might be able to share some tips and boost their sales a bit. Each person has their own strengths and weaknesses; teach them to play to their strengths. Foster teamwork. That's it. It's that simple.

One day, a long time ago now, my sister was making a call and mis-dialed. She and the person on the line started talking, and he asked her to come into his office the next morning for a job interview. She didn't have to work and wasn't job hunting, but she thought she'd go down and see what it was about. It turned out that the company put on job fairs, and the prospects were military officers getting out of the service. They were matched up with recruiters from Fortune 500 companies. The job involved lining up the recruiters who paid a fee. With no formal sales training, my sister was top salesperson within 2 years. She overheard the owner comment one day that he'd been trying for 7 years to get the FBI to participate and had gotten nowhere. She asked if he would object to her trying. His comment was that he'd buy her anything she wanted if she managed to get them. She called the FBI recruiter who was cool and disinterested until she started asking what traits he was looking for and how what she had to offer would fit his needs to perfection. End result? The FBI became a regular account. My sister was awarded a new mink coat at the next sales meeting. The coat wasn't the motivator, though. The fact that she could help the FBI and her employer was. In one of their sales meetings, one of the senior salesmen asked her how it was that she was outselling everyone-including him. She said, "Well, when you fellows approach a prospect, you act as if he has your money in his pocket, and you want it." It was her philosophy to help out the prospect, and it took her to the top.

I have another interesting story about taking care of customers. A company called a regional sales meeting to inform everyone in the district of a new corporate policy. The man in charge of the meeting told the salesmen that the corporation would no longer furnish technical assistance to accounts that didn't buy $100k each year. Instead, the small accounts would be given a phone number to call, and someone would help them that way. If that didn't work, and the salesman went to look at their problem, the customer would be billed for technical assistance.

One of the regional managers blurted out, "What stupid SOB thought that up?" Unfortunately for him, it was the speaker. A week later, that manager, after 20 years of service to that company, was let go. A week after that, he was working for the company I worked for. He brought all of his business with him. Then, he went out and got more of their business. A year later, the company that he had previously worked for was scrambling to do damage control. The damage: the business they lost over the manager they fired. Arrogance is an expensive trait in business.

Helping people with their business is the best way to build your own business. I'm looking at this from one perspective because that's what I'm used to. I've been working in the same field for some time. The truth is, though, this is universal, applicable to most business types. Helping the customer get what they need, what they want, with care, is the only way to keep your business running strong over the long haul. That person will be back, and they will send others your way, even if they never specifically state a referral. People are biologically wired to need connection, and, if you spend the time to connect with them and develop a relationship, chances are excellent that they'll be back. It's a win-win.

7: Poor Managing vs. Good Managing

Management style starts at the top. The CEO in a corporation sets the tone. The second tier of managers key in on what the head person wants. They anticipate what is expected and will usually tell the head person what he wants to hear. Arguing a point with a CEO or telling him what he needs to hear all too often will put an executive out into the job market quickly. Kill the messenger.

Below the CEO and his 'right hand man' are figurehead managers who seldom have the authority to make any decisions of importance. All lower level managers are there to see that everyone conforms to the corporate model as it is interpreted by the CEO. Everyone stay in your boxes. If you don't, we'll chase you all over the office. When we catch you, it's back into your box. If it's a minor infraction, you'll get off with a lecture. Don't make a habit of it, though.

The management of a business or corporation is crucial in how well it operates. There are examples of good management practices and bad in every organization. Unfortunately, for the most part, the bad far outnumber the good. Here I want to talk a little bit about managing done poorly. We'll get to some ideas on how to do it right further on.

What drives a poor manager is usually total self-interest. They have their agenda, whether it's to get to the top or do as little work as possible while they're on the clock, and they're going to do what they have to do to achieve it. They're always wondering what to do to make themselves look better today.

They are not team players. They'll suck up when it's time, but, the rest of the time, they have little compassion or interest in others, contrary to the smile and positive looking exterior. They are usually mentally nimble when it comes to dodging anything they have done, or failed to do, that would reflect badly on them. Pass the buck, plead ignorance, blame circumstances, blame one or more employees under them, backstab others by sowing seeds of dissension, lie. They will steal credit from coworkers and employees when it suits them. They know the company only needs so many people on the payroll. They will do what they have to do to be one of those who will be kept. These personalities have tickets for everyone, but they're for under the bus.

Poor managers let their emotions drag them around, whether they will admit it or not. Most of the time, they don't even realize it. They want to feel superior, and, the fact is, most of their decisions are made to support that. Though, they may be able to see a flaw in others (and usually despise it), they will not see it in themselves or will rationalize around it. They don't let reality mess with their ideas of superiority, and they get angry and defensive when questioned or when they feel threatened. They bully their subordinates and other managers in order to look like they have everything under control.

They command others instead of lead them. Because of this, they never have rapport with their employees. They comment, usually sarcastically, or argue about every little thing. They often take things exactly the opposite of what was meant if it dents their fragile ego. They are ruthless against anyone they see as a threat and tend to dislike working with people who appear smarter than they are.

These managers tend to copy what they've seen other managers doing. Because they don't get any real training (corporate propaganda, situational, and widget training don't count), they have to rely on monkey see-monkey do.

They very quickly learn to cover up their screw-ups. They see the other managers doing that. They learn how to keep the right people around them to help do this (but will probably eventually turn on those who helped them out). They also learn very quickly how important it is to pay lip service to all the right things (they learn what those things are from their peers). The good of the company, the good of the customers, the good of the employees. Some of these managers are not even aware they are playing this game, but others do it intentionally.

Many learn how to play the game. Instead of making decisions, they know they have to stall or defer. This makes everything move extremely slowly in a corporation, but that's okay, the manager covered his a**. They learn how to wage turf battles, how to encroach on another's turf while staunchly defending their own, how to influence others without any real authority to do so, and on and on.

Generally speaking they are complainers, criticizers, excuse finders, and blamers who are very negative with almost no can-do in them. Many are ambitious, sporting inflated egos, with specific agendas they are trying to carry out, in spite of competency level (or lack thereof, as the case probably is). They shirk responsibility, get involved in interdepartmental dissension, and generally make a nuisance of themselves.

Worse, though, is what they do to their subordinates. They don't support them. Most of the time, they don't even want to know what they think. They don't want anyone to know that they don't have all the answers. (Which is just idiotic since no one can know all the answers.) They tend to dump their work on their subordinates so they will have more time for politicizing. Subordinates can never really give an honest opinion because it could cost them their jobs. Employees are almost never fooled by the phony smile these managers have screwed on. Those that are initially taken in learn very quickly not to trust them.

This makes for a very uncomfortable workplace. Intimidated employees are uptight and very hesitant to make any decisions, even ones that will benefit the company. They often just don't have the energy to deal with the possible fall out from their manager. They will tailor their behavior according to that manager's mood, just to make sure they don't set them off. They know which managers allow what type of behavior. If this one allows creativity, if that one has to be carefully fed the answers, if this one expects them to stay crammed into their little box. They know that a strong disagreement with a poor manager could end their career, even if they are right. They also know that they have to make some decisions in spite of what management would say, because they have to do their job and can't bring themselves to follow some of management's more ridiculous orders.

Most companies succeed in spite of themselves rather than because of themselves. (Yes, I repeated myself, and I'm going to do it again because this warrants repeating.) The reason is that the people at the bottom, the wage slaves, and lower level management, can't bring themselves to do some of the stupid things they are ordered to do because it could or would be a disaster.

People, these types of managers are a cancer. All of this drama is way more than any good employee wants to handle. These managers run their best employees off, and who is left, all too often, is mediocre or worse. It will then take 5 people to do the work of 2. Passive resistance becomes rampant and is impossible to combat. Passive resistance is where an employee does everything 'by the book' but nothing seems to get done right or on time. Most of the time, they are aware of their actions and their effects. You can't criticize them because they 'followed the rules.' This is a way of getting payback against a poor management style.

A true example will help illustrate this. An order went out to shipping to ship 5 pallets of 5 gallon jugs. The shipping people knew they only had 4 full pallets and half of another. They shipped 5 pallets! That's what the order called for. The fact that the order wasn't complete was intentionally ignored. They filled the order as it was written.

Minimal output is the best you can expect at that point. All of these box people are 'busy' eight hours a day. Walk through the office, and watch them. Actual contribution may be far less than 20% efficiency, but no matter. A high producing manager in this environment is an endangered species. This is because they can see all the stupidity around them and just plain can't handle it (they eventually end up leaving). The other managers very often feel threatened by them.

Poor managers aren't engaged in the team or the tasks. They feel as if they are above all that. That hurts the team, and, at that point, they are the weakest link. Of course, they don't think so. (Side note: you'll never get an idiot to admit, or even believe, he's an idiot. The human ability to twist reality to suit their fancy is phenomenal.) Managers are usually paid good salaries because of their positions. If most were paid what they were worth, it would, in itself, be a great savings to the company because too many of them would only be worth half the government decreed minimum wage.

I heard a story from a friend about an occurrence in a hospital department. There was a very productive worker who got more done in a day than most of her colleagues combined. The mouse for her computer broke. Instead of replacing it, the manager told her she had to make do with what she had. They wouldn't buy her a new one... Thus, her productivity dropped down to the level of her colleagues. Where is the sense in that?

Now, some managers think that their job is to manage everything in an orderly and predictable manner. Pretty much anyone can manage objects. How many chairs do I need around the table for the 14 people expected to show up? How do I keep track of supplies? How many widgets should I order? That's the easy part. *A manager's real job is to utilize human resources.*

You have to be aware of their cost and contributions, but they have to be seen as individuals and as a group. It's not a memorization exercise. Guidelines are just that-guidelines. They can help keep you on track, but they cannot tell you what to do in every situation. There is no cookie cutter approach to working with people.

Managers are people too, and two of them may use the same management style, but it will look different because it will become individualized, specific to that manager. There is no universal "best" style of management. Some people never open their mouths, and their organization runs smoothly. Some people never close their mouths, and their organization runs just as well. A manager has to develop their own style. They can't copy someone else's. They'll find it doesn't feel right to them; others will know that it's phony. It just won't work. Good managers don't try to impress people. The more you try to impress people, the less impressed they are.

Here it is essential to know yourself. You need to know what makes you tick, what makes you crazy, what makes you focused. The best managers are those that are honest with themselves about their strengths and weaknesses. This will show up in carriage, and people will see it. Even if they don't see it, they'll be able to feel it. Confidence is key, and that's why working within your own style is so important. If you know where your energy comes from, you know how to tap into it for the good of the people under you and for the company.

Never treat hourly employees as inferior. It's not unusual for some of them to have more potential than you. Use it to everyone's advantage. Encourage individual development and never hold an employee back because you don't want to lose them. They will slack off or go to work somewhere else. If your workers are viewed as inferior, they will know it. The best managers surround themselves with people who are, often, smarter than they are.

Good managers lead rather than boss. I never tell anyone to do something if I can get them to do it by asking politely. It is an implied directive, but it's not abrasive. Asking also leaves open two-way communication. A good manager maintains the ability to see the bigger picture but is well aware of the importance of employees who do all the things necessary to make a company successful.

Good managers know themselves and are comfortable in their own skin. Because of that, they are aware of their emotions and how they can trip one up. They keep emotions out of the business decision making process. The focus in on their customers and their workers. An excellent example of this is Hobby Lobby Company. Their philosophy has always been to take care of their workers and customers. Much of their decision making about what they should stock comes directly from department managers of the individual stores. They have intimate contact with their customers and know what they would like to have available. The buyers look at these recommendations allowing the stores to key in on trends often before competing stores are even aware of them.

There are plenty of examples of good managing around if you look for them. For example, one of the largest, and possibly the best, heat and air service companies in our city doesn't advertise. Their technicians know their business. I have seen them tackle a cobbled-up system with components made by several different manufacturers and change only what needed changing. When they handed you the bill, the system worked and would keep on working. Each of their technicians is a self-contained, self-managing component of a large company. No micromanaging. You always get a fair price from them.

You are not responsible for raising your workers. It's not your job to be their parent. They were hired to do a job, a job that contributes to putting money on the bottom line. Manage don't boss. Once the staff is trained, it's just dumb to come in every morning and tell them how to do their jobs. You need to see to it that your people have the proper resources, coordinating where necessary.

A good manager is careful not to let their emotions drag them around. They know that emotional decisions and business do not mix well. They recognize their emotional responses and learn how to control them. They are always open to suggestions, even when it is difficult. Arguing and defending yourself may make you feel better, but it won't get you any closer to solving a problem.

As a manager, you have to have courage. Courage to admit when you are wrong, courage to face a problem head on and deal with it instead of just hoping it will go away, courage to admit when you don't know an answer, courage to bite your tongue to keep from micromanaging, courage to take responsibility for your actions and the actions of your workers. The list goes on and on. You have to be able to relax, even in a high stress situation, so that you can look at the challenges clearly and unemotionally. Never panic. The mind works much faster if you can stay calm. Fear and desperation are very common motivators in the management world. Don't let them make your decisions for you.

Keep an open mind. Never think that others have to perform a task exactly as you would do it. They have a way that works best for them. As long as they get the job done, and done well, does it matter how? If you can't stand to watch, you can always leave them alone to do it. When you think something is really important, make sure you've stopped to assess. If someone has offered a different idea, and you have a defensive or angry reaction, check yourself. A good manager will not respond quickly with a negative. Listen; hear them out. It might be a horrible idea. Thank them for their input; don't criticize. It might be an amazing idea, one you can implement. Whatever the idea, you will have built a bridge instead of burned the foundation of one.

We live in a fast paced world, and changes are guaranteed. A good manager expects that and constantly turns those changes to their advantage. Multitasking comes with the territory. You have to be able to prioritize and focus on what you're doing to get it done quickly and efficiently, while at the same time constantly reshuffling the needs of the whole throughout the day. You will also have to stay calm. When a manager starts to panic or lose their cool, the workers feel the shift, the whole atmosphere will change, and productivity will begin to decline. Your mind should be able to constantly shift between macro and micro throughout the day. This is a tall order, I know. That's why there will never be a surplus of good managers. Too many want a stable job that falls into a routine. That does not happen if you are managing people. There is not going to be a perfect day. That's ok. If you know you did your job to the best of your ability with the knowledge and resources available to you, you should feel great about that. That's all anyone can do.

Nothing of any size or importance is one size fits all. People come in all sizes, shapes, intelligence levels, and social/cultural outlooks. Whether those people are the workers under you, the suppliers you come into contact with, or customers is irrelevant. It's the manager's job to take all that and more into account and look at the big picture. You have to take into account things that are happening in your domain and align it with what's coming down the company pipeline. Implementing too many changes at once, however, means that work may not get done consistently or to a high level. Consistency is key, and it often takes time to teach each new initiative to your people. Follow up with them until it is habit for them before you go on to something else. Re-evaluate over time. Some things that make sense now might not in six months or a year.

It's important to keep things simple. Your operation will run much better. If something makes sense, then do it. If it doesn't, then why would you? Stop and think before you act, instead of reacting from force of habit. Consider all angles. Anything worth doing is worth doing right, and, as cliche as that sounds, it is true. This sometimes requires making difficult decisions. If you don't know what a manager above you would say about it, but you know you have to do something now, you have to make the decision you know is best for the company in the long run. All rules have exceptions. The thing is, to make decisions like this, you have to make sure you have your moral compass pointing north. Basic ethics are extremely important. Good management techniques are the most productive way to operate, and the foundation of those is good ethics.

It's a manager's job to know that most things that will go wrong today should have been fixed yesterday. If you know your job and your people, you will be able to see potential problems before they arise. Cutting them off at the pass is much easier and less stressful than trying to stop them full swing. Stopping a merry-go-round after the first push is much easier than trying to stop it when it's going full speed. Learn to be proactive instead of reactive, and things will go much more smoothly for you and for everyone under your supervision.

I know there are so many working parts to managing, most of which are not the moving parts but the people, especially now that there are so many generations in the workplace at once, and you have to learn how each one communicates, acts, and even thinks differently. It can get stressful and overwhelming. Learning to enjoy your job, though, will make it much easier. Look for the positive and have a sense of humor about the wacky antics that go on around you. If it's not getting in the way of business, what difference does it make if the office clown is trying to balance one of those cone cups of water in his ear? If someone wearing an old t-shirt to clean out the back room doesn't bother anyone, then why reprimand that person? A loose, relaxed, positive mind will find solutions to the small issues that pop up during the day. That will make work, and life, much easier and more pleasant.

8: The Most Difficult to Manage

Looking at the larger picture, I always end up at one conclusion. The reason the corporate model fails is this: business decisions are made based on emotion, not on reality. Emotion-based business decisions are almost never good. (This is not to be confused with intuitive decisions based on years of experience and proven results.)

What are emotions? My definition might not totally fit the dictionary one. I view them as primitive hereditary responses, most having to do with social interaction. These emotions were already bred into us before our ancestors came down out of the trees. What I mean is the innate, self-interest/self-preservation instinct that colors everything we do and feel. Examples: a desire to fit into a group (be it social group, family group, or even a nation); a desire to have power over others or be a member of a ruling group that has control over "lesser" mortals; a desire to protect one's family or friends; a desire for revenge; desire to be praised by your social group; a desire to assume something is true when, in reality, it isn't; a desire to measure up; a desire to feel secure. I'm not saying these are bad. I'm just saying these desires have sway over every decision we make if we let them.

Allowing yourself to react out of emotion instead of objectivity can be a disaster in business. Say, for example, you're trying to get a new piece of business. You bid a job too cheap for fear you won't land the business. Only, you end up with the business and find you are selling below your actual costs. A major company in our market had bid a large treating job a couple of states away far too low. It was so bad, they came to our chemist to see if he had any solutions that might at least allow them to break even.

In fear you are giving things away. Competitor's love that. Then there's the other side of the coin. You have a small account that depends heavily on you for material and expertise. You charge him unfair prices because greed got ahold of you, and you thought you could squeeze a little more out of him. If he goes out of business, what is going to happen to your sales? You were chasing rainbows and one of them snapped back and hit you in the butt.

Emotional managing doesn't consider the dollars and cents (ie profit) component. Surrounding yourself with people who are going to always agree with you because it makes you feel more secure is not going to get the work done or pay the bills; and you're deluding yourself if you don't believe at least one of them is just there because he wants your job. If you get an idea that will make you look great, but you don't do your homework about cost and market, you could potentially waste thousands of dollars of company time and money just because you wanted someone to pat you on the back. If you build a machine, one that was, in fact, necessary to the company, but you refuse to take suggestions from the people who are using it because you feel they aren't smart enough to question your design genius, that's another example of being dragged about by emotion.

So often, power is a club wielded because of ignorance, fear, or arrogance. Forcing others to do things in an exact way because it makes you feel more in control, more secure, is just another example of managing by emotion. The emotional managing that is the bureaucracy in the big black box is all aimed at one objective: reduce everything to a system that always works perfectly. Then you'll never have to worry or be afraid. That won't work. It can't. Uncontrolled emotions (including the fear/insecurity that begets iron fist control) are like unruly children. Do you want Dennis the Menace running your company?

Here's the thing: everyone has emotions. Seems obvious enough, I know. The difference is that the good manager knows how to respond to them. He acts instead of reacts. Reacting is damaging in social relations. In business, it's expensive. Sound business decisions are based in reality, not how you feel about the situation. Every business decision has an impact on profit. You have to be in charge of your emotions, not the other way around.

That brings us to a very important point. One of the most important points, in fact. The most difficult thing/person that anyone ever has to manage is themselves. One of the best things you can do for yourself in business, and in life, is to spend some time in serious self-reflection, to take a personal inventory. Now that may seem a little "self-helpy" and not relevant to business at all, but you cannot manage others effectively if you cannot manage yourself.

Now, I'm not saying you have to tell anyone you did it, but taking a self-inventory is an important step in knowing yourself, knowing how to control your emotions. In fact, it's probably better if you don't discuss it with others.

What are you truly afraid of? Do you feel you have to put on an act for others? What was going through your mind the last time you became very angry? What do you hide from others? Why? Do you seek power over others? Why? What makes you feel good? What gives you a sense of accomplishment? Do you like or dislike most people? What is your source of energy? What is your management style? Are you organized or unorganized? Does work get done because of you or in spite of you? What is the turnover rate under you? What is the quality of work you get from your workers? Is there any theft under you? Do you have an eye for details? Are accidents a normal occurrence (in terms of broken equipment, etc. as opposed to personal injuries, although those count too)? Do you have repeat customers, or are they always new faces? Are your workers loose and comfortable, or are they stiff? Do you have standards for other managers? Are you an alpha, or are you totally subordinate? Are you a people pleaser, or could you just not care less? Do you get it done, talk it to death, or put it off? Do you finish what you start? Do you take time to do things right, or do you avoid it until you have to slop something together? Do you have a good imagination or none at all? How do you handle stress after work? How do you handle the stress at work?

This is not a moralizing project. It doesn't matter to me what the answers are. No one is ever going to know. If you're brave enough to do it, that's good enough for me. If you find out that your sole purpose in life is to make others happy so they'll like you, ok. If you find out that you have a mean streak a mile wide and have no desire to change that, don't even think it's a bad thing. Ok? This is all about enlightened self-interest, about knowing yourself so that you can control your emotions when making business decisions, especially as it relates to people.

Self-confidence is essential (not to be confused with arrogance which is completely useless). Ambition is only a dirty word when it is misused. You can't be a manager if you don't have ambition or drive of some kind. That's what got you where you are or is getting you where you want to be. Knowing your strengths and weaknesses is the first step to be able to manage effectively. You'll be able to play to your strengths without wasting time trying to overcome weaknesses (or shortcomings, if you prefer). Which is, oh by the way, the exact opposite of what you're taught and what you're evaluated on in a corporation, go figure. An alligator watching a squirrel run up and down a tree might wish that he could do that. The fact is, no matter how hard he practices or tries, he's never going to be able to match the squirrel. Going the other way, if he plays to his strength, the gator is king of his domain. Folks, life is a come as you are party. It's less a case of what you have and more of a case of what you do with it. I'm disgustingly average, but I've always tried to use what I have. A church billboard caught my attention years ago. It read "There is nothing more common than un-realized potential." How true that is. And how sad. Utilize what you have without focusing overmuch on what you don't. If you learn that you want to make a few changes, then that's ok, too, but it's not the purpose of this evaluation. Ultimately the objective is for you to be comfortable in your own skin. Those who work with you, for you, know how you view yourself. They will notice when you settle into who you are.

There are still going to be those stressful days, those trying times. You have to know how to handle it. It's a killer and will take years off your life. When someone says something to you that causes a flash of anger, it means they are hitting close to home on something, and it's time to dig it out and come to terms with it so it won't trip you up. This work can pay huge dividends in the end.

I'm average on IQ, but I try to use what I have. If subordinates are smarter than I am, that's great. I'm going to utilize their talent so we all win. (One day that guy may be my supervisor.)

I recently had to give a presentation to the management of a prospect. The people I worked with on the project laid out a step-by-step approach, complete with slides. I didn't have time to memorize it, and I know me. If

I had, it would have been stilted and boring. Instead, I stood up and stated our findings, identified the problem, and gave them workable solutions to improve their operation. I had to be me for it to not feel awkward. (We did get that account, in case you were wondering.)

I'm not telling you to do anything I haven't done. I have insights on this self-research. I spent a few years around AA as an Al-Anon. I have spent a good many nights at open AA meetings listening to people's stories. I have witnessed the results. I know how hard it is to get honest about who you really are. You can't do it for someone else, even for your job. You have to do it for yourself. For the AA person, it's a matter of life or death. If they don't get honest, they get dead.

You have to be your own critic. Few employees are going to criticize the boss to his face. Your friends will seldom let you know your faults. It's human nature to try and please the boss. Remember the old parable about the king's new clothes? It's very easy for an owner or CEO to feel smug and all powerful because no one around them will let them know they're riding through town on a horse buck naked. How have you related to others? How could you have handled a situation better? Did it turn out that your approach was actually win/lose, or was it truly win/win? Should you have been more forceful or more compassionate? No one likes even constructive criticism from others. It's not nearly as distasteful if you do it yourself. Empathy is the ability to put yourself in someone else's situation and imagine what your reaction would be given the same stimuli. If you were the person you just told to do something, what would have gone through your mind? Those who develop themselves become truly capable of bigger jobs, promotions.

Here's the kicker. You have to know yourself. You have to play to your strengths and minimize your weaknesses. You have to evaluate yourself; you have to be critical, but you shouldn't beat yourself up. You're going to make mistakes; you're human. It's not worth abusing yourself over. Get up, dust yourself off, adjust course, and move right along. You'll be better for it. Your company will be better for it. Your employees will be better for it, even if they don't realize it. Know Thyself. Control your emotions. It's the most difficult thing you'll have to do. I've been there. I've done it and am still working on it. Emotions are sneaky devils, and they will bite you when you least expect it.

I've come to realize that few people recognize their emotions because they never realize they exist. Most people use self talk that becomes unspoken thoughts. Unrealized are the non-verbalized thoughts that come from emotions. A manager demands an employee stop work and sweep up a few pieces of paper and gets angry because they try to reason with him. The worker will start the end of the shift cleaning in ten minutes. It doesn't matter to the manager. They ordered something be done, and it's not negotiable. That's bossing. No thought was given to the order of 'do it right now'. It was emotion driven. No thought was given to how the order might be received by the employee or even if it was reasonable.

Why the knee jerk reactions of "don't question my order" or "do as you're told, period!"? What's the basis of the reaction? Insecurity, fear, power? Was an order even necessary? What was the employee doing when a snap decision about the paper happened? Was the employee trying to finish taking care of customers? If so, the employee had a better concept of priorities than the boss. If nothing were said and the manager checked 10-15 minutes later and the paper was picked up, it would be fine. It's a manager's responsibility to decide how they will respond to emotions. Are they going to react, letting the emotions control them, or are they going take control of their emotions and act logically? The distinction may seem subtle, but it can mean the difference between the survival and the death of a business.

9: Finding People. Training Them

I always say, "A mediocre or poor hand is worse than no hand at all." I know you've seen evidence of this. I know you've wondered about at least one employee: "What do I pay them for? They don't do anything." Finding good people takes time, but it is well worth the effort. People are what make a business run. Good, well trained, ones will make your business successful.

First, you have to find them. Where do you look? Everywhere. The grocery store, mechanic, in the oil field, casual encounters, fast food places, inside your current organization (a bit more on that later), applicants. It doesn't matter where you find them. It's all about their work ethic and potential. If you have enough applicants, your chances of getting good quality hands are much greater.

I'm not going to go into depth on the interview process other than basics. That's really all you need. There isn't a perfect interview. Forget the script and focus on what you need. Make sure to read between the lines. Don't look for perfection. Don't help them or hinder them. Be careful. Everyone always puts on their best faces for an interview. Make sure to listen not only to what they say but also what they don't.

Review their work history. (I've found that those who started work at an early age are among the better bets.) What type of Jobs have they held? Have they done anything related to the job you need filled? Do you think they're going to be comfortable working in the position for which they've applied or the one you need them to do? Are there gaps in their work history? Do they list "personal" as their only reasons for leaving employment?

A good way to put an applicant at ease is to start with their early employment or school activities. This is usually nonthreatening and can get them to relax and open up a little. Then move into finding out about them by asking open-ended questions, staying away from yes/no questions. Control your emotions, and don't react to what they say. Maintain a pleasant countenance. If there is a pregnant silence, don't bail them out. Wait and see what comes of it. It may be nothing, something inconsequential because they're nervous, or they may be trying to hide something. Consider all possibilities.

Suck-ups are very smooth interviewees. They will try to read you and feed you what they think you want to hear. If in doubt, lead them on a tangent and see what comes out. You just might get them to expose themselves. This might seem like a waste of your time. It's not. Consider how much of your time they will waste after they've been hired, whether it's because they don't actually want to do the job, because they're trying to take over your position, or any number of negative traits.

Another very important thing to remember is that you shouldn't hire someone just because you like them. They have to be able to do the job and get along with others. You have to be fairly certain they can do that, otherwise you're letting your emotions run your interviewing process. Also make a habit of interviewing on a regular basis. Don't let yourself get too far behind. That is when you are the most vulnerable to making poor hiring decisions.

A manager may not always be able to find the quality of people to interview that they would prefer. OK. You still have a job that needs doing, so take the best of what's available and try to get their best performance.

When I entered the army, I had three years of college behind me. The basic training cadre went through the files for each new trainee as soon as they arrived at boot camp. Files were pulled for anyone with prior service, ROTC, etc. These trainees were assigned temporary sergeant ranks and operated the training company under the supervision of the drill sergeants. I was assigned as squad leader of the first squad in the first platoon. Somehow they figured out quickly that I could handle strange personalities. By the third week of boot camp, all of the strangest in our 200 man company were moved under me. Ten men. We were getting gigged badly at weekly inspections. Individually these fellows were under-motivated and just didn't care. I'd had enough. I called them out behind the barracks building. I reminded them of what our head drill sergeant said the first day. "Gentlemen, I can't make you do anything, but I can damn sure make you wished you had." I informed them if they didn't start helping each other and getting us through inspections, I was going to volunteer our squad for every shit detail I could find. They took it upon themselves to shape up, and we got through it. The whole was greater than the sum of the parts. I didn't tell them one thing about what or how to. They did it themselves as a team.

If the quality of the available help is not so good, you still have to get the best performance you can and get the job done. You have to be a leader. Not one of those eight balls in my squad would have done anything if I had tried to order them around and criticized them. It's human nature, an emotion, to not like being told what to do. I never tell someone what to do if I can get the task done by asking them to do it or finding a way to motivate them to want to do it.

Don't be quick to hire people because they are "experienced" in the job you need filled. I will take a good trainee any day over a mediocre or poor experienced candidate. The mediocre hand will rarely get better and will become even less productive over the years. A good trainee will usually pass a mediocre hand in a few weeks and will continue to get better. If he stays in an hourly job, he will still be paying his way right up to retirement. Often, though, the good trainee develops and moves up in your organization.

Try to hire well. Never hire a person out of sympathy. You will get a poor, nonproductive employee. You are running a business, not a day camp. Anyone you hire must contribute to the bottom line. At least 80%, and maybe as much as 90%, of personnel problems can be taken care of at the hiring point. Allow yourself to be picky, and choose employees carefully. Once you hire them, they are your responsibility. You owe them training, a mentor, a fair shot. If they cannot perform their job to the standards necessary, you owe it to them to scoot them into alternative positions to try to save them. If you can't, or they just won't cooperate, then don't keep them, but never make this decision with any haste.

I'm going to talk about hiring managers for a bit. The process is a little different than hiring hourly employees. All of the above still applies, but there are more things to consider. When you check references, make sure to get any "inside" information you can via people who worked for them, suppliers that you know had dealings with them, etc. It's a small world, and there is usually someone who can give added insight. With a little creativity, you'll be able to find someone who can answer some questions for you, someone who is not under legal obligations to only state neutral or positive information. Then, there's always FaceBook, Twitter, and YouTube. This manager is going to have a large impact on your business, so, again, be choosy.

There are many pros and cons to hiring people with experience, and this is amplified in management positions. If you get a good one, it can be a real boost to your company. Unfortunately experienced managers may bring with them some undesirable habits and practices from their previous experience. This could turn out badly, so be cautious.

Hiring non-degreed management trainees is becoming less and less common, but it is still viable if they are carefully selected (in this instance I specifically mean ones who are currently outside of your organization). The big thing here is their work history and track record. Any motivated, intelligent person has the potential to be a good manager if properly trained, guided, and supervised.

Hiring college graduates is the norm nowadays. All too often this is an ego thing on the part of the person hiring. They believe that, because the person has a degree, they are in some way more competent than someone without one. The problem with this is that, many times, a degreed person entering the job market is only a trainee. A degree only gives you an overview. They are taught the theoretical world of management. The "in a perfect world" rules of engagement and tactics. They learn how to manage the tangible, the quantifiable. Managing those things is only part of the job. The other part, the larger part, is managing people, which are not quantifiable at all and are very often unpredictable (widgets don't move on their own and can't speak). When the new graduate starts the new job, they have to be trained or train themselves on the details they need to know in order to earn their keep.

Here is the problem. Many graduates have no experience dealing with the "real" world. Starting in the lower grades, and all the way up through a degree or degrees, people are fed information. To make the grades, they are taught to turn around and regurgitate that information back to the instructor in the way of tests. The bulk of the graduates have had little experience in managing, even managing themselves. Often they are poor trainees because of the superiority complex having the degree has given them. They are skilled in memorization and filling in the blanks, but they are often not skilled in managing on the fly.

We were asked by an oilfield management company if we could take a dozen summer intern engineer students for a week. This would give them some exposure to our specialty. We had work to do, and we took them to the field and put them to work. We observed them and concluded that, of the twelve, only 2 of the boys and 1 of the girls were likely to become good engineers. Another girl was probably there because someone told her she should become an engineer. She showed little interest and little aptitude. The rest of the boys, it was apparent, had one interest. Get hired by a big corporation and start moving up the ladder to their comfort level. Actually working and doing a job was a low priority.

Hiring friends and family is a disaster waiting to happen. If you must, because of very, very good financial reasons, it must be done carefully. It should be made clear that the relationship on the job is different than the relationship outside the job. They will be expected to perform as well as anyone else who would fill their position. Favoritism is a morale killer for the rest of the workforce, so they will get none. Be aware if they try to take advantage of your relationship. More often than not strained family relations or the loss of a friend is the result of this. Seriously consider that before you make the decision to go ahead and hire a friend or family member.

You've done your interviews; you've done your hiring. Now, those new employees are your responsibility. What are you going to do? When an employee is hired into a typical corporation, they are given the normal propaganda orientation about how wonderful the company is to work for, the great surroundings, the good management, growth opportunities, etc. At McDonald's in the 1980s, this was done with talking chicken nuggets… Unfortunately the training often consists of little more than the aforementioned blather. Folks, get rid of that and get into the nuts and bolts. In some industries this means OJT (On the Job Training). Delivery drivers learn from current drivers. Technical jobs, depending on the industry, may be an apprentice situation. In some industries it can mean seminars and workshops. Whatever the case, make sure that you take your responsibility to your employees seriously. (Remember they will live up to or down to your standards and expectations.)

You'll have to work up a training program for your hourly employees. If you already have one, that's great, but look it over to make sure that it truly suits your needs and is realistic and actually useful. Define the job clearly and teach them what they really need to know to fill the role. It is incredibly frustrating for a worker to go into a position with half-a** training. It drops morale quickly, overwhelms the employee, and can cause a loss of efficiency and, possibly, the employee. In the medical profession, young doctors work under older physicians for several years before they work independently. Stated another way, a new doctor has a mentor. In some jobs, a new employee is assigned a mentor such as a senior experienced employee to guide them in their learning period. Many times, unfortunately, there is no mentorship, and that is a detriment to the employee and the company.

A probationary period is extremely helpful. It gives the manager time to assess if this person has a can-do attitude, if they are teachable. Be aware that people learn at different rates and in different ways. Sometimes a slow learner turns out to be exactly who you needed. A fast learner may not be. They may get bored easily and be ready to move on before you can accommodate them. Stay tuned into them during probation so you can catch any characteristic that will not be good for the long haul. Keep emotion out of this. If they are a good worker, but they're a troublemaker, is it worth it to you to maybe lose some of your other employees? Troublemakers never fit; get rid of them.

It is important to note here that different generations think and act very differently. You cannot expect someone in their forties and someone in their twenties to have the same mindset, values, and priorities. You cannot expect them to learn at the same speed or learn things in the same way. Keep that in mind when you are evaluating them during a probationary period.

Don't immediately tell trainees what they're doing wrong. Show them how to do it right. Lay the foundation for confidence. I usually tell people I need them working with me, not for me. If they work for you, they are wage slaves and are obligated to do the minimum to get from clock-in to clock-out. If they work with you, it puts them in a team situation. Keep in mind, however, that it is not a company's, or a manager's, job to raise people. If a trial employee shows undesirable traits, and an unwillingness to do anything about them, get them out of there.

Only you know your exact training needs for your hourly employees. The fact is, though, that training is necessary. You don't know what your new hire doesn't know, and they don't know what they've never been taught. Figure those things out, help them be successful in their new job, and you will have added value to the company.

Good managers are a must. While getting a good recruit is most of the battle. The rest is training. They must be trained well and oriented to manage as opposed to micromanage. First, you have to define the job. They have to know what is expected of them, just as any employee does. It's just as frustrating, if not more so, for them to walk into a situation where they weren't given the proper tools to do their job to the best of their ability. They have the added pressure of having people under them who are depending on them that may be adversely affected, as well as the bottom line as a whole.

Unfortunately most managers have had to learn by trial and error. They have gaps in their performance and in their people skills. They've also learned by what they observed their past supervisors doing. Just as unfortunately, they have, most likely, been copying someone with no training and, very possibly, picking up some bad habits.

Most management programs/training teach managing situations and material assets, not people. These programs emphasize managing the tangible, the quantifiable. When it comes to the human aspect of managing, they are handled in a similar manner as everything else. People should fit into nice, neat, little boxes, so they can be easily controlled. It is an illusion that managers following the corporate model buy in to. It's not a wonder that new managers make mistakes. It's a wonder that they function at all.

Some people have what would be termed "natural leadership qualities." That's a huge advantage. I have a brother-in-law like that. His father was an Air Force pilot, and they moved often. He had been in twenty-two schools by the time he graduated from high school. He had to adjust and adapt quickly. He could walk into a room of strangers, and, without making any overt move to gain attention, everything would be revolving around him within 30 minutes.

Most of us have to learn or be taught the skills necessary to manage people. Your training program should be heavy on teaching your recruits how to manage the people and light on how to manage the objects. People are always moving, their moods are always changing, and they do not like to wait.

New managers will need to be trained to handle the basics of human interaction, and you need to be comfortable in the knowledge that you can support the decisions they make so that they feel empowered to do just that. New managers need to learn multitasking, flexibility, and rapid change. They need to have courage to face their employees who may be posing a problem or situations between employees without deferring responsibility up the chain. They need to know how to set goals for workers and motivate them positively to get results and how to create a dynamic team to increase the profitability of their division and the company overall.

Good training may seem unnecessary. Why do you need to pay to train people to make other people feel good? What does that have to do with business or profit? Be careful of underestimating the impact of poor management. For example: you own a gas station, and a road customer stops in. The whole store is tense because of the manager's attitude toward the employees under him, and the place needs a good cleaning. The employees are passively resisting doing their jobs, so it's taking three times as long as it should. This particular customer may only be using this route once, or he could be a regular along this way and this is his first stop in your station. Will he come again? Maybe, but he won't make it a point. Same thing with the next customers who come in. If the service were better, you could have gotten repeat business. If you have a good manager who knows how to get the best out of their people, these situations could have gone very differently.

With a little creativity, you can have a training program created or find one that will teach the essentials of managing people, of getting the best from those who work under you. If you haven't acquired the ability to give people training, there are companies that can step in and help with that.

Training costs money. Money you may not feel like spending. The truth is: it's an investment. At first you may only see pennies on the dollar because of the training. Over time, though, it will continue to grow. Good training can create good managers. Good managers can create a positive, energetic working environment. A positive working environment will increase productive output of your employees (not to mention create an attractive environment for customers). Productive employees do more work in less time and with a better attitude (treating coworkers and customers well). What does that equal? Money on the bottom line. Enough said.

10: Current Employees

You've hired them, and you've trained them. From now on, employees will need to be frequently evaluated. Not the official employee review, but an ongoing informal evaluation to keep your information fresh and realistic. Why? Some will need to be moved to a different role, some will be promoted, some will just plain need to go. If they aren't truly contributing to the bottom line, you don't need them. Keeping your company staffed with solid people decreases turnover, because people will know that they can develop their potential and that they work for a great company. It also increases productivity. Both of these things add money to the bottom line.

Keeping deadweight, useless employees costs you big time. I've seen a few new hires that it was apparent within in a few days they were highly allergic to work. They were kept because the people responsible didn't have the courage to let them go. People like that cost you. If you have too many of them, it threatens the jobs of those who are good workers. Is it right to close a business and put good people out of work because you didn't have courage? What about the good people's families?

If an employee won't do their job, let them find a place to work that is better suited for them. That said, you never fire someone on a whim. Your actions will have a direct impact on your other workers. If the person has a family, it will directly affect them. Consider moving them to a different job if that will fix the problem. If, after an impartial evaluation, you have to let them go, understand the impact on the rest of your employees. Few people are going to feel badly about you letting a poor hand go. Getting rid of them will raise morale and help the bottom line. On the other hand, if you let a good worker go simply because you didn't like them, or they told you what they thought instead of what you wanted to hear, it will be known throughout your organization within an hour or so. You don't have to like someone if he puts money on the bottom line. The only requirements are: they do their job well, and they get along with their fellow workers. If you get upset at a good worker, go take a good stiff drink. The water fountain is just around the corner and down the hall.

A point here. You seldom have to fire people. You can allow them to fire themselves. You call them in and explain the unacceptable behavior and give them a reasonable time to correct it. If they don't, give them a final warning. The third time, you give them their last check. Additionally, I observed an interesting phenomenon when I worked in a personnel department. If we did hire a poor worker occasionally, it was, often, not necessary to fire them. The work force was superior there, and they resented a poor worker. After a couple of weeks of no one talking to you except as necessary for business and no one sitting with you at breaks or lunch, you'll get the hint. They were almost always gone long before the expiration of their probation period.

Does the employee you're evaluating get along with other employees? Are they upbeat and generally pleasant? Do they normally get their work done right and on time? Are they team players? Are they organized and neat? Do they do more than the minimum required for their job? Are they a doer, not apt to complain when it's necessary for them to work past normal quitting time when you need them to? If the answer to these questions is yes, acknowledge them. Let them know they are doing well. Hold on tightly to employees like these. If the answer is no, you'll know what to do.

A note here. Any successful company can carry a few employees that can't hold their own and should do so. You take care of longterm employees who are in failing health. Let them work as long as they can make some kind of contribution. Adjust their hours, working place, etc. Their knowledge, experience, expertise, and customer connections have a direct impact on your bottom line. How you treat them will be observed by the rest of your employees and will have a direct impact on work force morale.

Another note. Don't overstaff. People work far better if they have a manageable load. This means they usually have something to do every morning. A normal workload means that occasionally there is no immediate work that has to be done. Let the workers organize catch-up work, housekeeping, paint the walls, whatever. Everyone be useful but relaxed. It shouldn't last long before you will get thrown back into ten hour days and some weekends. Most of the time eight hour days will be the norm. My personal rule: only add a worker when you need half a worker or more, and the workload will likely be increasing.

If you are evaluating an hourly employee for a management position, there are a few more things to consider than the above questions. Promoting from within can be a fantastic idea. Probably 90% of the time, a good trainee will make a better manager, for the long haul, than an "experienced" manager, as I've said. They know the company, the job, and the people.

For these managerial candidates, you need to know what drives them, what motivates them. Do you think they'll be able to make the switch from hourly to salary? Are they going to be able to maintain a professional work environment with people they may have been peers with before? This is, many times, the toughest transition to make and requires a high level of maturity to pull off.

Watch out for BS and flattery. Make sure they aren't being promoted according to the Peter Principle. Are you considering this person because you like them or because they are truly qualified? Management is no place for pets, and not everyone is management material.

When making an internal promotion, I highly recommend it be done on a temporary basis. Tell the "new manager" you need them to help out by managing a function temporarily until you have time to assess things. You know, maybe eliminate the job, or merge the group into another department. Use your imagination. Don't give them a raise if you can avoid it at that time. Let them do the job, and, after an appropriate time, assuming they do well, find out if they're OK with supervising. If they are, give them a raise and keep them in that management job. If it was apparent the person wasn't going to work out, put them back where they were. They don't lose face that way in the eyes of their fellow workers. A small bonus of appreciation would be appropriate.

Evaluating managers is a whole different ballgame because of the strength of the impact they have on your organization. When it comes to evaluating managers, you have no friends or family. Don't zero in on a stereotype of a "management personality," and think they will be the best. Some of the best run companies I've observed were so laid back you had to ask who the CEO was.

You have to back off at arm's length and question what they are doing and why. Are they taking care of the people they are over? Are they taking credit for what their workers have actually done? Are they claiming credit for the ideas of others? Do they encroach on another's turf instead of working with other managers to benefit the company as a whole? How did they get where they are? Whom do they associate with? Did they ride someone's coattails up the ladder? Do the people under them work for them or with them? Did productivity increase or decrease under them? If in doubt, talk to former employees or get a current view of them by way of a third party. Individually, do they contribute to the bottom line or take away from it? Can they be retrained?

Look at what they offer. Is it really significant? Is this how they should be using their time? Does what they offer belong in their area of influence? What have they really accomplished? Have they completed projects? How important were they profit-wise? Was the focus to make themselves look good? Are people who work under them happy, relaxed, and above average in accomplishing their tasks? Did they earn their position or was it given to them because there wasn't anyone else to fill it? Do they get things done?

Are any of these people trainable? How many of your managers need to be replaced? Can you do without a manager in that position? Can some of them be moved elsewhere? How many in your accounting and engineering departments need to be moved out? Are some of them salvageable?

Observe who wants to keep the floor in a conference or conference call. What are they really saying? If, in listening carefully, you find they are speaking in glittering generalities ("we are working on" "we are planning on") instead of the concrete facts, question it. Are they taking a long time to say little or nothing? Is that their personality? Maybe they don't understand a need to focus on what is important by organizing what they plan to say. If that is not the case, however, and they really are just blowing smoke, then they probably aren't really contributing to the bottom line. You have to watch out for them. Listen to see if they're telling you what they think you want to hear-exaggerating the good and glossing over the bad.

Does this manager almost magically appear anytime the big boss is around? Do they make it a point to be seen by the head man and attempt to carry on a conversation with him whenever circumstances permit? Have you ever stopped to listen to one of these conversations to see what the motivation might be? Managers who are just about making the climb play the "game." They are experts at sucking up and not making any mistakes (aka taking no risks) and socializing with the "right" people. These people are very good, however, at covering up their screw-ups.

On the other hand, people who are doers usually don't like conferences or conference calls. They are usually thinking about the dozen other things they could be doing instead of being tied down listening to people ramble on inconsequentially. If they do feel that they have to contribute something, it will usually be short and to the point. In fact, some of these people are seen as having little to no personality by people who don't really know them.

Say you have a high producing field salesman. They get overloaded and can't take on more business unless they have hourly people assigned directly to them for support. These salesmen are excellent managers. They are not into emotions; they're too busy and focused to have time for such foolishness. They are focused on getting the job done, not on their subordinates looking busy eight hours a day. In most cases, their subordinates are worth two or more micromanaged hands, because they are led, not bossed.

Most of these field managers would do an excellent job as a top manager except they are too valuable generating sales. No one stops to look at that. If your best managers are not available, what do you have left to work with?

If you are assessing a manager, find out how he manages from the people under him and place yourself mentally where they are. Would you want to help someone who lets you know they are superior to you? The dictatorial manager comes across as a good fellow to people on his level. For those above him, he is always trying to impress. For those below him, he makes sure they don't question any of his rules. He makes sure his underlings reinforce his self-image. Any who indicate otherwise will not be around long. It's been my experience that those who want power the most are the ones that are most poorly equipped to use it. Some of this type are not even very bright. They will use all of their limited resources, however, to climb to the top...

In his book, Lee Iacocca mentioned Chrysler Corporation had 17 VPs when he took over. He tried to salvage them, but he was only able to retain 2. He didn't go into details as to why, but I can hazard a pretty good guess. Many had multiple secretaries and held sway over kingdoms of underlings. Power is intoxicating, and they were completely inebriated, not able to give any of it up. They will fight every attempt at changing anything they control. That has been my observation over the last several decades.

If you have to use cheap tricks to motivate your managers, you need to examine why you have inferior managers. You can't pay poor mangers enough to turn them into good managers. This is especially true for sales. It is highly recommended no incentive bonuses for upper management. All focus then goes on the bonuses instead of the customer. Pay sales managers well and expect them to do their job instead of turning them into commissioned salesmen. Commission salesmen are a disaster in a service oriented company. Anyone ever consider that managers are nothing without the workers? They are only part of a whole. When emphasis of bonuses is based on total dollars, forget margin and profit. If you simply trade dollars and don't make money, you won't stay in business.

One day, I watched while a sales manager refused to accommodate a customer because he was afraid they would request a credit; it would have kept the upper management from getting a bonus for the quarter. It cost nearly a million dollars in sales over the following 12 months and permanent ill feelings with the customer. Due to a lot of effort on the part of a salesmen, however, the business was regained. (This is rarely the case.)

A few hundred or even a total of a few thousand dollars for bonuses verses a million dollars worth of business? All focus is on immediate reward. For them. Forget everything else. Forget R and D. Forget customer and long range market development. Forget employees. Heck, forget the company itself. The truth is: workers are a lot smarter than power managers think. It's left unspoken, but, when people are being used, morale plummets and the bottom line shrinks. If you do believe bonuses would be beneficial, they need to focus on objectives. Team bonuses would be preferable to individual ones. Company-wide are better. Think this through carefully so you don't motivate part of your company and have a negative effect on the other parts.

I'm not big on RHIP (Rank Has Its Privileges). It fosters arrogance which, in turn, breeds poor decision making. Every employee expects managers to earn more than the hourlies, but the hourlies also understand they are part of a team and so is the manager. All too often the only ones who don't understand this are the top management. They see themselves as bosses who have power over all underlings. They take full credit for anything good and blame everyone else for any and all shortcomings. They are gods. Don't question their decisions. What is lost in this approach is the fact that it takes a whole organization to be a business. Top management doesn't operate the business alone. They have to have the people below them to carry out all the functions. If they could do it alone, why waste money on all the other employees? If the top managers deserve a bonus, so does every employee in the company.

A little history here. The worst abuse of slavery was the treatment the slaves received from the overseers of the plantations. The land owners lived in cities and contracted out the management of their plantations. The overseer was paid based on profit. The quick fix was to starve the slaves and let them make do with rags for clothing. When they didn't work hard enough, beatings were used for motivation. Anything for that bonus. Fast forward a couple hundred years. Employees often have to work with damaged or subpar equipment. They are belittled and treated poorly by managers. If they don't work hard enough, they're threatened with a pink slip. Oh, but at least they get paid… I hope you can (relax, open your mind and) see the parallel and the complete abuse of power by a poor manager (very often driven by a bonus).

Evaluate your hourly employees and your managers often. Don't use the results to beat them up. Use them to honestly assess their value to the company. Keep in mind that most people can change for a short period of time but, more often than not, will fall back into their old habits relatively quickly. If they do, they are going to become liabilities once again and drag down the corporation. That said, acknowledge those who deserve it. Get rid of those you don't need. It's simple. Not easy but simple.

11: Knowing is Half the Battle

I've talked a good bit about evaluating and gauging what you have. I want to talk a little bit more in depth about some of the types of people you will see in management. This will help you to be more aware of them and spot the little things that will help you create an honest and accurate evaluation of your management team.

There are several management types that are a complete hinderance to the profitability of a business. When these types get into positions of power, it can be a complete disaster. It might not look like it at first, but, in the long run, they will destroy a business. In evaluating your managers in a stagnant company in trouble, you will find a sizable block of NO men who make minimal, to no, contribution. There will also be a number of lazy managers, apathetic ones, micromanagers, number crunchers, and power-hungry cutthroats. In this soup, though, you are likely to find some very good managers who haven't been able to fully demonstrate their potential or haven't been given credit for their loyalty and contributions.

I want to describe some of these different management types. The objective is that you'll recognize them when you see them. It will be much easier to evaluate them if you can see them for who they really are and assess the impact they are having on the business, whether it is positive or negative. Remember that this is not the end all and be all of lists. Its purpose is to start you thinking.

Lazy managers generally only copy what they've seen other managers do, especially ones they've worked under. They don't take the time or energy to figure out if what they're copying is working or not. They are quite content to stay in their little box.

These managers like it when others stay in their little boxes, too. That's all they really know how to handle. Generally speaking, they like to hide behind paperwork because it's "easy." Dealing with the actual managing of people, which are changeable and varied everyday, does not appeal to them. They'll chat with their subordinates, but when it comes to actually managing them, they don't want to do it. They'd rather just put in their hours and go home. They don't want to waste time and energy on problems they might actually have to think about. They aren't too lazy to blame all the issues on someone else, though. They don't think ahead; they can only deal with the issues that are in front of them at any given moment. They aren't fond of helping people out. After all, isn't their job as "boss" to "boss" people around and make them do everything?

One of the funniest things I observed along these lines involved a person promoted to "manager." No training. He took this promotion to mean he was a boss. What does a boss do? He bosses. He had one subordinate. He would sit and order his one subordinate to do all the physical work while he did absolutely nothing. In another instance, the "manager" was continually interfering with their worker to the point where they had to hire another person just to get the job done. You can bet the "boss" liked that. The more people you command or have under you, the more prestige you have within the corporation.

Apathetic managers exhibit many of the same characteristics as lazy managers. They just want to sit there on the time clock and get paid. The major difference is that they don't care one bit about the business, their actual job, or the people they manage. Their subordinates pick up on this. With the lazy manager, the employees might like them personally and do what they say because they're a likable person. The apathetic manager, on the other hand, is generally disliked, and people will only do their jobs to the bare minimum. This is very destructive to the work environment and the actual profitability of the business itself. Remember: people don't care about people who don't care about them.

Unfortunately, as an organization grows, the current corporate model dictates that you will lose control unless you make everything rigid. This causes the rewarding and promoting of micromanagers.

Little regard is given to whether these people can actually accomplish anything of use. The criteria for their promotion is that they seem to not make mistakes. They also tend to project the image of what people think is leadership.

Micromanagers feel secure because they know how to control their environment, or so they think. They spend their time making sure that everyone is following corporate policy down to the letter. Oftentimes, they are one of the driving forces behind the instigation of more rules. Every company edict is just one more notch into their belts. It makes it look like they're doing their job. All their little minions are treading the mill, exactly how they should be. Exceptional people cannot survive in this environment, and they won't try. It only makes it worse when the micromanager is sometimes lax on one policy or another because they're not paying attention and, then, at a different time, starts to reinforce it again. This is confusing to employees, not to mention annoying and unfair. It can potentially lead to a lawsuit which definitely takes money away from the bottom line.

This brings us to the number crunchers. Again, this has it's place in the workplace. Numbers and hard facts are an integral part of business. The problem comes in when people who are purely numbers oriented get into management. Generally, these people are completely concrete with little creativity. They are intelligent. They can make the grades and usually have a degree (at least one). The problem: they tend to reduce the world around them to manageable boxes, including the people they are managing or even the customer. They can get very angry or upset when things don't fit into the boxes they've created for them.

This type of personality in management is a roadblock to the company's success. They tend to believe they are never wrong. Numbers don't lie. The math is sound. Therefore, the employee questioning them must be wrong. Case closed. That employee will get the "you're stupid" treatment from then on out. They also tend to be negative and suspicious of people and their motives, oftentimes considering everyone a thief, and often have little (to no) people skills. They aren't diplomatic communicators and can alienate their subordinates with their superior attitude. They try to project themselves as the watch dog of all corporate funds and nothing should be done without their approval. They drag their feet and are very slow about making decisions, if they make them at all. They have absolutely no sense of handling sales, production, or people.

If an engineer in charge of the development of equipment is this type, they tend to get emotional about their projects. Once they design something, they don't allow changes. Even if it is evident to everyone around them it's poorly designed, they will never see it. Even though their design is going to cost the company in a lot of ways (initial production cost, inefficiencies, unnecessary labor, high scrap rates, frequent breakdowns, etc.), they don't see that either.

A true example from a friend of mine: A large oil field service company built all of their own specialty trucks. These were designed by a team of engineers and were beautifully done. When a new truck was needed at a branch in the field, one was built and delivered. Even before the unit arrived, the warehouseman ordered a long list of fittings, valves, and pumps. As soon as the truck came in, it was completely taken apart and reconfigured. When it was taken to the field, a week later, it would actually work. Nothing was ever said to the people at the corporate office about this because it had already been tried, and they were informed that the engineers were smarter than any field people. All the parts that were surplus were stashed in a corner to gather dust for a few years and eventually ended up in a junk yard. (My friend was the warehouseman that ordered the needed parts.)

When accounting is taken over by this type of personality, it is like building a concrete wall into the organization. They become completely focused on saving money, pinching pennies. They will cut wherever they see an opportunity. This includes inventory. Inventory control is a must, but it needs to be done realistically. Producing and overstocking slow moving merchandize is just plain "not-bright." The 80/20 rule often applies to inventories as well. 80% of your sales will come from 20% of your product line. The other 80% of your product you look at on an individual basis. If you need an average of 2 widgets a year, don't produce 6 of them and tie up money for months on the other 4. If you need more, then produce it as needed to cover unexpected orders. Maintain reasonable quantities and have them available. The lazy empiricist doesn't look at anything that can't be simple numbers. Try selling customers what you don't have and telling them accounting won't even restock until they have an optimum order quantity—I bet you can guess their response. This also includes quality of merchandise. If they can get raw materials cheaper somewhere else, they will. Again, I bet you can guess the customer's response and the response of the employees that are affected down the line by the lower quality.

Numbers people are so focused on pennies that they can't see the dollars in front of them. The focus on cutting costs just perpetuates the cycle. Cut costs, lose customers or clients, have to cut costs more, lose more customers or clients, etc. That doesn't even include areas within the organization where they are cutting. Employees won't be able to get what they need to do their jobs. They will be laid off, or their hours will be severely cut. This will lead to bitterness and resentment in the ranks.

Numbers people can't see these things. They are so busy trying to keep the numbers in the balance book at an acceptable level that they don't consider what those numbers mean and what might be done to raise the top line number without reducing the other numbers. They never see any context for what the numbers are quantifying, and, worst of all, they don't care. You never see a number cruncher out in the plant talking to workers. Finding out what's going on in the real world is inconvenient. Everything has to be their way. Reminds me of a kid I stopped playing with when I was little...

Next, the climbers. These people really get my goat. They apply at big companies solely to land the job and climb to the top. Starting on day one, these people already have an agenda and go into the workplace and get the lay of the land. Immediately they find the one in power, a mentor on whose coattails they can hitch a ride up the ladder, or the one they would like to influence. Then it becomes a game. The end goal is to win—to get to the top. The goal for right now is to get the next level. Then the next, then the next.

These power-mongers are, most of the time, very sorry managers. For one, when a manager's objective is to gain and hold as much power as possible, they don't want anyone around them that might tarnish their self-image, so they surround themselves with flatterers and "yes" men. They also don't want to have any subordinates who might challenge their power. For the rest, he'll use his power like a club, quick to invoke the name of a superior to bully others. "Don't question me, I'm in tight with the top people." They treat their employees as if they are dumb, lazy, and should be told what to do everyday. Everyone has to fit into the neat little box, should respond as expected, and stay in line. It makes him look better. They will be spending a lot of time trying to impress their boss, all the while shirking any real responsibility they see as "not my job." Their attitude is not company, employee, or customer oriented. It's all about them. Once these ambitious managers get a taste of power, they're intoxicated; they spend their time trying to stay on that "high," and they will often make poor decisions in pursuit of it.

It's not uncommon for this type of manager to make a mistake and fire a subordinate, claiming they were the one who messed up. They'll do anything to avoid getting a black mark on their record, anything for their ambition. Oftentimes, when a manager like this goes to the boss with a good idea, it's because he's claiming credit for someone else's idea. Sometimes one of his subordinates suggested it to him; perhaps he overheard someone talking to someone else, perhaps even one manager to another, about a way to increase output or productivity or a way to make a job easier. If the idea makes it to the bigger boss, changes are implemented, the blindly ambitious manager gets credit for it. I know of a case where a very competent young man worked with a fellow that he thought was OK. He found out years later that the fellow was running him down to their boss and also claiming credit for his work. What happens to employee morale and the environment of the workplace in cases like these? Passive resistance sets in, employees no longer openly discuss ideas, and there could be a high turnover rate for this department.

I've had dealings with this type of personality before. A man like this was hired into a company I worked for, and he figured he could recruit me as a useful tool. He invited my wife and I to meet him and his spouse for dinner. As soon as we got into our car afterwards, my wife said, "If he had complimented me one more time, I would have barfed in his plate." It was a clear example of the phoniness of these people.

A couple of weeks after I started work as a janitor at the machine shop, I was visiting with the building maintenance manager. He asked me, "Do you know what happens when you get to the top?" I said, "No." He said, "There's only one way, and that's down." Turns out, at one time, he was the main plant foreman and had bulled his way to the top. He had an awful management style. Even though he worked at that machine shop for over

20 years, I never detected he had a single friend out of the 300 hourly employees. This fellow had a couple of years to go before retiring. He was lucky to be kept on that long. The man who displaced him was every bit as cut-throat but was a smoother politician. A few years after I moved on, the plant manager while I was there got moved out by (of all things!) his own son-in-law.

How about another story? When one of the companies I worked for was being taken over, one of the upper management men pulled me aside and told me I was going to have to change. He loaned me a book to read. I took it home and skimmed through it. It was basically a how-to book on climbing the corporate ladder. It advocated being friends only with people who would help you move up. Once you passed them, you no longer socialized with them. You latched onto a rising star and rode their coat-tails up.

I returned the book the next day, thanked the fellow, and told him that it didn't fit me. He said that he hadn't expected any other answer but did say that I would be hard to replace if I left. To them, loyalty and hard work were commodities that they could buy and sell. I had my résumé ready a couple of days later, and I moved on. They ended up having to hire three salesmen to replace me.

The self-centered power seekers are loyal to no one. They are cut-throat opportunists. Their primary objective is power and importance. You better believe that their subordinates know it. For them, everything is focused inside that big black box. Their ambition and all of their goals are packed in there. They lose sight of the market, the employees, customers, everything. If they mess something up, it's swept under the rug, or they blame it on a subordinate or, better yet, another manager.

As the power seeker moves up the ladder, they're so busy trying to get promoted that they don't even bother trying to learn the job they were hired to do. Because of this, they tend to have a shallow or superficial understanding of their job, knowing just enough to be dangerous. As a result, they can make stupid, expensive decisions. They'll find a way to pin the blame on someone else, though. They leave no base below them on their climb. All they leave is a trail of angry, and perhaps even broken, people in their wake.

My brother had just started work as an aerospace machinist at North American Rockwell. The workers already employed told him that his new boss was a real "hard case." My brother didn't care. He went to work and did his job. After a few days, the manager would stop and visit with him. One day one of the climbers in the department spotted the manager and my brother together and walked out of his way to do a little sucking up. After the fellow moved on, the manager told my brother, "You never promote a guy like that, because he's always looking for the next job." Translated: People like that usually don't do their current job or even have the knowledge they should have. I have seen them move up the ladder, though.

What is missing in too many of these type of people, besides intelligence and competence, is a basic set of values, i.e. ethics. Everything is for them, and they have little or no regard for others. Make no mistake, they can spout compassion, teamwork, good of all, etc. along with the best of them. They have about the same commitment to these high sounding ideals as most politicians. Their sheep skin is always handy. These managers can be devastating to a company. Unfortunately, it is usually in such a subtle way that no one seems to notice. Or maybe it's just because the people above them are the same way.

Then, (finally) there are the good managers. Good managers tend to be team oriented, not glory hogs. They don't just preach team work; they practice it. They have no qualms about giving credit to the right people for ideas and work well done. They are oriented to think, "What can I do to make things better for subordinates, customers, and/or other departments." They tend to know who they are and what they're about. They also don't really believe in sugar coating the truth. They're honest. Don't ask them anything if you don't want the answer. They are careful, however. If they don't believe that what they have to say will change anything because of the management above them, they will usually try to stay quiet. They're not going to lose their job because someone doesn't like to hear the truth.

A good manager has imagination and mechanical aptitude in the sense that they grasp concepts of the job and how to use them. When they encounter a problem, they assess it as it is, look at the history or origin of the problem, then look at possible solutions, and consider the long term consequences involved in those solutions. They consider every factor they can. Cost and results. Now and later.

This is just an overview, but I think you get the idea. Knowing some of the behaviors and patterns of the different types will help you to figure out who is who. That is essential in any solid business. Management will make or break a company. Put in people who will make it great.

12: The Black Box

The whole objective of the corporate model is to make everything completely predictable and completely controlled down to the smallest detail. Because of this, all power is concentrated at the very top of the management hierarchy. No one below the top is allowed to make significant decisions because they are considered inferior, not smart enough, or just incompetent. To make sure that everything and everyone is under control, they are smashed into boxes. Even if one manager has to sit on the lid while another one nails it closed.

Micromanaging is usually driven to the very lowest level of the company. There are petty rules for everything and the paperwork to keep track of almost anything at any given time. The managers that are between the hourly employees and the top people are reduced to YES/NO men. Anything the top dogs want automatically gets a "yes" answer, whether it makes sense or not. Going the other way, anything requiring a decision automatically gets a "no" answer or is put off indefinitely. The problem with that is that people who excel in fanny kissing often can't manage a one-hole outhouse, much less a division of a large company.

To most corporations, dealing with the world outside the black box is just damned inconvenient. It's necessary. After all, you do have to have money coming in so you can keep the doors open. You have to buy materials and maintain equipment, though. Oh, yes, and make payroll. Customers don't always follow trends or work in predictable patterns. They are seen as an annoyance and treated as such. There are days when traffic or the weather doesn't cooperate with the set plans. These normal day to day inconsistencies of life interfere with the internal corporate games. Suppliers and service companies are treated like thieves. Even a loyal service company that has always gone the extra mile in the past may get dumped because another company has underbid them by a fraction of a percent. Service is all too often done poorly or grudgingly. Even sales and profit can become inconvenient because the numbers do not always fit into neat little boxes.

Most companies prefer that people stay in those little boxes as well. They stack on the rules and policies, making sure they don't act in any way unexpected. Exceptionalism is frowned upon and/or punished because it is uncontrollable. They would rather have 10 mediocre workers doing jobs that 2 or 3 exceptional people could handle because those 2 or 3 people might be eccentric and try to get outside of their boxes. They would rather have people who just go to work, do what is expected, and leave. The actual amount of work getting done might be minimal, but that's ok because it is comfortable and predictable to work with people who are going to do the minimum to keep that paycheck coming.

What about the managers? They, too, have their own boxes. Slightly different, although not much, from the hourly employees. Few are given training. If they are, it is partially company propaganda that the corporation wants them to believe. The rest may be a poor management theory spouting the way the corporation wants them to behave. (Any relationship between the company propaganda and reality is purely coincidental and any usefulness derived from the management theory will be mostly accidental.) As long as they act in a way expected by their managers, though, everything is fine.

Everything about the corporate model, however, is designed to destroy morale and initiative. There are no rewards for hard work and creative thinking. There is only punishment for mistakes. Keep doing the minimum, take no risks, be a "friend" to the right people. CYA. Even peeking out of your box carries consequences. Whether it's threats to be boiled in a vat of low cholesterol frying oil or getting a pink slip. Basically, to put people in boxes and keep them there, you have to reduce them to humanoid robots, running on a single, specified program. This turns the work environment into an incredibly oppressive place. (Not to mention unresponsive and, in turn, unprofitable.)

As in a dictatorship, any show of independent thought and action is a threat to management. The thing is: dictating from the top down to the bottom of the work force ensures poor morale and no teamwork. There is no hope of good morale when the individual is not allowed to have a say in how his job is done. They can only work for the company. Do as they are told and nothing else. They are not allowed to work *with* the company.

People at the top have no clue what is really going on in their ranks. All the information (that is not purely numbers) is filtered through the suck-up in the levels leading up to the top. The top might have a vague feeling that things are not quite right, so they'll start preaching teamwork and playing the "rah, rah" game. They plaster the walls with teamwork signs, have company picnics, fundraisers, anything to try to raise morale. At that point, that's like putting a bandage on a broken spine. You can try. For all the good it will do you. That, too, becomes a waste of time, resources, and money. Those activities smack of paternalism and thinking workers resent it. I know of few people who like being patted on the head and talked down to.

This all translates into lethargy. Everything about the corporate model impedes anything of value getting done. What happens to get done is done slowly, and high quality is not a requirement. The first reaction to any request is "no" or "how can I put this off until I examine it for any risk it might carry for me." This results in a bloated (and rotting) organization where it takes 2 or 3 people to do one job, and, even then, it is not likely to be done well.

Everything seems good to the casual observer, though. Every employee and every manager fits perfectly into their designated boxes. Everyone is busy eight hours a day. You can pretend you don't see that guy a few rows down shuffling the same stack of paper back and forth to different sides of his desk taking the time to look at each one intently for a few seconds like he's actually doing something important.

The corporate model as it is practiced has a huge flaw that everyone overlooks. (Or perhaps they just plain don't see it.) Almost every poor business decision I can think of was made based on emotions instead of cool, logical thought. The need to make everything completely predictable, to control everything, is based in emotion. Usually arrogance or fear. The interesting thing is that most people are not even aware of these emotions.

The result is that they let their emotions drag them through life and color all of their decision making. Perhaps for a single hourly employee at the very bottom rung, allowing this to happen doesn't have very far reaching ramifications (though it does have some, make no mistake). For the people at the top in a corporation, however...

Whether the top people in a corporation are being controlled by their arrogance or their fear, and possibly a toxic combination of both, the result is very similar. They usually turn into bullies. They are quick to let underlings know that rank has its privileges. They are bosses, not leaders. They treat people poorly and make decisions completely colored by whatever emotion it is that drives them. This is a disaster of the first order. The company is headed for oblivion on the fast track. The sad thing is that they don't even seem to realize it. They see leaks here and there, but they think that filling them with silly putty is a good way to stop them. If you're reduced to forcing people to put up teamwork posters and having meetings about putting more fun in the workplace, your ship is sinking and fast. Wacky Tacky Tie Day will not help you turn a profit next quarter.

That's the big black box. Everything becomes focused inside it. The ambitions of dozens, perhaps hundreds of people. The behavior of hundreds more. The idea of the way a business "should" run. It all becomes completely internally oriented to the point where the corporation gets completely lost in that box. They lose sight of the market, their customers, their employees, and everything that actually makes the money. It becomes completely rigid, unable to adapt to changes in time, market, and people. Eventually it will collapse on itself.

But! We did everything by the book. That same book most other corporations are using? If you wanted to succeed, you were reading the wrong one. There is a better way. What is it, you ask. Read on. I'm going to spell it out for you.

Part 2

How It's Done

13: How to Do It

The corporate model looks good on paper. Everything has a place and a function. Use of people is well defined right down to the individual jobs. The human factor has been removed. Morale is nonexistent, though. Treat them like machines, and they will perform down to your expectations. Everything in the stagnating corporation is designed to slow up or block anything useful being accomplished.

Most companies following the book eventually choke. In the marketplace, when a competitor is no longer in the game and is being shut down or sold, few people really examine what went wrong with them. Blame game, finger pointing, scapegoats, but you seldom hear the whole story. The direction for an organization is set at the top. Call them President, CEO, Operations Manager, or any other name that seems appropriate. By the time most CEOs in large companies reach that level, they have become very effective politicians. They are adept at reading people and learning what will influence them. These skills are used to the CEO's advantage. This would not be a bad thing, only, all too often, there is a dark side that shows up to go with this. Power is an intoxicant. There is an old adage "Absolute power corrupts absolutely."

The power manager tends to surround themselves with people who play on their vanity. The top person only hears what he wants to. Questioning or disagreeing with the top man's remarks and edicts often results in the death of the messenger. No one crosses the boss and survives as an employee of that company.

When a company moves into this situation, the top manager is isolated and surrounded by Yes Men. What does that do to decision making? Even the most brilliant intellect occasionally needs to be reminded that everything they say isn't always wise.

What's going on down in the trenches? The workers, including lower levels of management, are isolated from the decision makers, and their opinions and morale are seldom considered. Big mistake. Good employee morale puts money on the bottom line; poor morale takes it off.

When employees are treated as objects rather than individuals, they have an extremely effective way to fight back. Passive resistance. They follow the rules and look busy eight hours a day. But things go wrong. Everything is slow. The usual fix is to add more layers of management and more employees. Things won't get better, and the added payroll comes right off the bottom line. Office staff are non-revenue generating employees, and this is usually where more employees are added. In order to pay for each new staff member, a company has to increase sales accordingly. I'm not sure that always happens.

While the bureaucracy is growing, the corporate manager's games are being played. I won't even get into this, there are hundreds, if not thousands, of books on that topic. Unfortunately most corporations follow a predictable life cycle, and eventually disappear.

Why?

Taken to the base cause: it is decision making based on emotions instead of objective thinking. Every business decision has an influence on profit. When the people running a company don't allow feedback from the real world, the end result is very predictable.

Once a corporation is set into these destructive patterns, it is nearly impossible to correct it. It would almost be easier to shut it down and start over. At that point, the bureaucracy is so suffocating, the people so set in their ways, there's almost nothing you can do. There is a huge resistance to change. Lethargy has taken over.

I did, however, say "nearly impossible" to correct. Not "impossible." I know it can be done. I was part of the complete revamping of an old company that was in trouble. I didn't really understand it at that time, but it's very clear now, and I understand why it worked. There were ten good years before the second generation manager died. (Then the third generation came in, were pushed aside by outsiders, and that was when I moved on, as I stated earlier.) You have to have courage and the ability to use your brain. First of all, though, you need to be able to recognize what isn't working. Not just the symptoms that spring up but the true cause of the "disease".

A company is like a person. Each part has to run well for the whole to be healthy. If one organ in the body shuts down, the rest have to try to pick up the slack, but it will never perform to peak again. If the tax on the other organs is too much, another will shut down, and on and on This happens in a corporation. No sales, no company. Sales but no products, no company. Products but no shipping, no company. Materials produced and shipped, but no billing, no company. No company, no work.

Most doctors will tell you that the way to stay healthy is to eat well, drink water, and exercise. A simplistic answer, it seems. Leonardo DaVinci said, "Simplicity is the ultimate sophistication." The answer is similar for saving a corporation. Simplify things, get back to basics. Let's get back to the basics of the way a good, profitable, "healthy" company should be run. Let's look at some alternative methods, methods I have observed to be successful over the years. I've gone over these a bit in the first part of the book. I'm laying it all out here without any fluff. This is where the rubber meets the road.

The fact is: change has to start at the top. The top manager has to have the courage to evaluate the organization honestly, without those emotion colored glasses, and make some tough decisions. They'll have to seriously review everything that's being done in the organization and why. Nothing should be off limits or sacred. Does it contribute to the bottom line in some way? If yes, great. If not, stop doing it. (This review should be done often to make sure everything in the company is still contributing to profit.) The top person will have to surround themselves with people with imagination and ethical ambition and allow them the freedom of dissent.

Minimize the layers of management. Honestly assess the need for each layer. If you truly need it, then keep it. If a particular layer is full of people pretending to be busy eight hours a day and has a manager with nothing better to do than sit on his butt and micromanage down to how many pens are in each holder on each desk, it's a safe bet you don't need that one. Don't be afraid to get rid of it. Shuffle your good people around.

Find a place for them. The rest? Let them sit on someone else's clock and bring their company down.

Occasionally these people with too much time on their hands come up with BS projects with which to pester the workforce. Mandatory surveys that are just plain stupid. But it only takes 30 minutes…OK. Only no one thinks of the transition time when a person changes from one task to another. Before an employee switches to do a survey, they have to shut down what they're doing. Then they have to actually do the survey. After that, they have to switch out of that mindset and return to their meaningful task. Think about the total payroll costs, matching Social Security, medical insurance, etc, then the actual hour of time they were paid. Multiply that times the entire work force. Was that survey really worth that amount of money?

That's for only one BS project. There are usually several of these each year in a corporation. More expensive than the direct cost is its affect on morale. Those busywork things are accepted by the workers with a groan and a few choice four letter words. They'll take the time to do what they were told, but, usually, with anger and resentment. They're trying to do things that have a direct impact on making the company money, and they have to suffer fools.

Obviously some projects are necessary. Be choosy about which you expect to be done. Consider the source of the idea. Consider the true economic ramifications for now and the future. This is a great way to cut costs without actually cutting anything. Employees will thank you for it.

Excessive communications are just that: excessive. And unnecessary. Do you need each and every form your company uses? Does it add value to the company or help to your employees? If it doesn't, do our forests a favor, and stop producing it. How many conference calls or call reports or email reports, etc, are really important? Do you really want to take time away from your employees doing their job just to hear that they're doing their job? Does that even make sense? No, it doesn't. It's annoying to your good employees, and it gives your poor employees time to blow smoke and procrastinate from doing the job you pay them to do.

Get rid of all your petty rules. Some policies are essential for an organization to run smoothly. Some are just another way of micromanaging. Some were just put into place because someone was too chicken to confront a subordinate. Do you really need those? Isn't it better just to hire managers with the courage to do their job? An honest evaluation, honest observation of how they are carried out in the workplace, will tell you which policies are necessary and which are just crutches for poor managers and poor employees.

Don't be afraid to spend money. The money will come in. Share it with the people who were responsible for making it: the entire workforce. No, I'm not saying give it all to them, but certainly reward them with good pay. You should be paying the best rates in your industry. After all, if you follow the advice in this book, you are getting the equivalent of 2 or 3 of your competitor's workers for each of yours, so paying more is not going to be a hardship. Some of the rest of the profits can pay for proper maintenance of equipment, scheduling capital improvements, and investments in R and D, to name a few.

If you feel that you do need to make some cuts, make sure you "dance with the one that brung ya." Seriously assess what it is that has made your company so successful, and be certain you don't do away with it in your cutting. Sometimes it's just one thing that can create a following, influence brand loyalty. That thing might be small, so make sure you don't overlook it. Cut with extreme care.

Lay out general plans of expansion and anticipate market conditions, but always be ready to adapt immediately to opportunities. I have seen several golden opportunities missed because of fear and negative thinking. Oh my! The market has dropped. Remember, where there is a will, there is a way. When there is a drop like that, assess what your competitor's are doing. Now look at the opposite and find a way to gain market share.

To most big corporations, sales are very inconvenient. I heard an accountant ask a sales department manager if there was something that could be done about the fluctuations in sales from one month to another. Short of calling your customers and telling them that they can only buy a certain amount every month or telling them to go buy from your competitors, there isn't a way to make the sales numbers fit into the box neatly. I know you're not going to do that, so you'll have to be flexible and creative instead.

If you want a great organization, and you're trying to change the one you have that is currently based on the corporate model, you will have to assess all of your employees. Are they each contributing to the bottom line? Are too many of them dead weight? Keep extraneous personnel to the minimum, especially office personnel as they are a non-revenue generating factor. If one person is capable of doing two jobs, such as EPA requirements and safety, let them do it. Even a modest excess of clerical help or dead weight employees is extremely expensive. Look at how many dollars in sales it takes to pay for any one non-revenue generating employee. Don't look at the office type's direct cost. Look at the money left after the cost of goods, overhead, taxes, etc. Take one individual paid $40,000 annually, add on the 1/3 hidden costs that go with it. $60,000! If you net 20% that will require $300,000 in sales. If you want to keep some profit, you have to add another $100k or more. Evaluate carefully and dispassionately. Ask yourself, do you need a 1/4 or 1/2 more worker? Consultants and temporary employees are sometimes a good answer. My personal policy has been to add another worker only when the job requires more than 1/2 another employee. Until you reach that point, just pay a little overtime or maybe work a little more yourself. You might moan and complain; but you're not going to fire yourself, so just suck it up and get on with it.

Identify which of your managers are good ones and which are poor ones by evaluating them objectively. Have they always agreed with you on every issue? Have they accomplished anything worthwhile? Have they always been careful not to make mistakes (to the detriment of the company)? Have their past business decisions been sound? How productive are the employees who work under them? Retraining will not always help because some people are not capable of leadership thus cannot be good managers. Management is no place for someone who is only good as a drinking or golfing buddy. If you are incapacitated and the manager you are evaluating will be put in charge of everything, what can you expect? Will you be secure that things will run well, and you will have no worries; or would you need to be looking into getting on welfare and operating on food stamps?

Of course you do need to train managers when it's needed. It can be in a seminar with a group. It can be in an office with only 2 or 3 managers and yourself, or one-on-one. It can mean sending them to a training program. Whatever works. It's not a matter of which method but what is appropriate. A slightly formal seminar by a consultant may be just the thing for 15 or 20 managers. Following that, some managers, especially the less experienced, may benefit greatly with some one-on-one mentoring. Stay away from all rigid management approaches that are one-size-fits-all. Encourage individual development, especially hourly people who are considering a move into management. A trained manager works more efficiently and helps their subordinates to do the same.

Staff all management slots with people who have owned and operated their own businesses or are capable of doing so. Team players only. If they can't play team sports, send them to your competition. Give your managers authority and resources needed to do their job. Give them the authority to make decisions, even about spending money. Then leave them the hell alone. I happened to turn on my car radio one Saturday while going to a hardware store. A reporter was interviewing a TV evangelist and asked why his organization was so successful. The evangelist said that, though it went against his very nature, he found that what worked best was pushing decision making as far down the organization as possible. An excellent commentary of what I'm trying to convey. The CEO should function as a figurehead and coordinator. The managers will handle all the day to day operations and will keep the top men informed of anything significant of which he needs to be aware.

Minimize management. Keep them focused on doing their job, too busy to be nitpicking their employees. If they have time to micromanage, either you don't need them, or you need to give them more responsibilities to utilize their spare time. At lower levels, where it's appropriate, the supervisor should be expected to help if his group is under the gun or short-handed. They do this mindful that they may have to stop and take care of their primary duties on short notice. These little things on a manager's part will promote true teamwork. Good hourly people will give you all they've got when you need them to, and one will usually outperform 2 or 3 box people on a daily basis.

You will have to realize, and remember, that the objective is to get the work done, not look busy eight hours a day. Most people prefer to be busy with meaningful work. It gives them a lot of reward, and the day passes faster. They feel that they are appreciated and are carrying their share of the load. They also understand that they are helping others in the company in keeping their jobs. Don't get all worked up because a worker doesn't appear to be busy. That's their supervisor's job to assess.

Don't let managers hold a good employee back because he's

"indispensable." That employee with potential and ambition will go work somewhere else where he can develop. It might be a competitor. Worse, he may stay, get discouraged, and regress to an average hand. Employee morale is a crucial factor, and good managers know this. The old machine shop where I worked was an oppressive environment. They had a good year if they netted 2%. The place where I worked for 11 years netted 25% plus. The key was a non-oppressive management style which lead to higher employee morale. Enthusiasm will permeate the whole organization. No opportunities will be missed. Competitors won't be able to match you, and you can take as much market share as you want. Good employee morale puts money on the bottom line, and poor morale takes it off. Do you want 2% net or 25% plus?

You need a stated goal for your workforce. Your entire workforce. A focus for them. My daughter found this in some of her studies. Many of the more successful companies have a simple, clearly stated goal. I like "The Customer is Number One." After all, without them, the company can't exist. No one gets paid. It instills a can-do into every job, and the organization as a whole. Every function of the company focuses on that objective. This automatically instils teamwork. Don't preach teamwork. That's condescending. Instead, truly practice it. Encourage it. This orientation includes every department and every level of management. Each worker should know that even responses and decisions from accounting often have a direct impact on customer relations, order processing, shipping, manufacturing, etc. *Every* department directly impacts the customer. With that in mind, everyone focuses on the customer. Encourage communications between all departments and all employees. To actually make it happen, stop bossing. The objective is to get people working with the company. Not for it. Forget the RHIP, and treat every employee with respect, especially the hourly workers. Listen to people! This is a poorly practiced skill that can work miracles when used properly.

With things structured like this, the company won't be bogged down in the foolishness of micromanaging. You will operate at a minimum of overhead because you can get full use out of every employee. This management style requires courage. This organization of people expects constant change and will adapt to it. Even so-called "bad markets" are often a great source of opportunities, and they will be able to find them. Can-do will be the reaction to any challenges.

One of the first things that may come to mind as you read all of this is that you'll have no control. Wrong. You'll find you have more. Good managers understand that the top people need to be in the know and will see to it. What will be missing is the minor, everyday happenings that have no immediate affect on the big picture. That frees up a lot of time on everyone's part, loosens the atmosphere, and creates an environment of teamwork. Perhaps this seems counterintuitive, but you will be amazed by the results.

If you plan to follow any of my advice, you will have to call your workforce together and tell them about the changes you plan to institute. They will feel that they are going to be a part of something great, and they will help you make it happen. Yes, there will be a few who won't like it. Give them a chance, but, if it's apparent that they are not going to get on board, make a decision. Be aware that some people are too insecure to work in anything but a rigid, predictable environment. During the transition in a change-over that I witnessed, similar to the one I'm suggesting, one of the top production managers couldn't change. He'd been there for 35 years and was set in his ways. They tried something. They moved him to another department, outside sales. Lo and behold, it was a perfect match. A happy ending. He had a job he did well, the other employees saw that he was treated with respect instead of immediately let go after such long tenure, and the company benefited.

With this model, your operation will keep growing. Usually there is no need to dictate from a higher level of management. Everyone is focused on a common goal, the customer, and that instills teamwork at every level.

We've covered some of the basics of creating a flourishing organization. There is one more thing we need to discuss before we finish. It's one of the most important aspects, if not the most important, of a good business.

14: Leadership

One factor that most companies lose sight of is the one that can make or break the business. They put their emphasis on numbers. Most of the things that lend themselves to this empirical approach are fixed or semi-fixed costs; however, taxes, government mandated requirements, even the cost of goods is very similar to what your competitors pay. What makes your company different? Why do customers go to you instead of someone else? Your prices influence that but only a little. The snazzy building might influence it, but, again, only a little. The thing that has the greatest influence is the one thing that management, very often, does the poorest job handling. The human factor.

Really great managers don't manage people. From the CEO to the lowest level manager, it doesn't matter who it is. The great ones don't manage. They lead. There is a huge difference between a manager and a leader. This difference is little understood because there are so few good managers, let alone great ones. Great managers, leaders, know how to develop their workers, to motivate them, to inspire them. They know the value of employee morale, team building, getting your employees to buy into the company vision, of treating people with dignity, and taking the time to earn respect.

That is a lofty goal, you might think. How does one even begin to accomplish such a thing? And why would they want to? (We'll get to that in a bit.) You do have to want it. You have to want to be a great leader to your people. Whether it is because leaders get more from their employees and, in doing so, add more money to the bottom line or because they care about their people is irrelevant (although truly caring about them does help because they will be able to sense the difference). Once you know that getting the best from your employees and helping them reach their goals (because they help you reach your goals and the company's goals) is important to you, you can proceed.

Earning respect has many different facets because different people respect different things. You must be knowledgable but not too proud to say you don't know something if you don't. That goes a long way in fostering trust and respect in your employees. You have to be approachable and ready to listen when people come to you with concerns. Yes, sometimes, they'll just want to complain. Hearing them out, though, if you have the time, goes a long way. This is a balancing act because you have to know when to stop them so you don't get dragged into their personal problems (you are not their parent or their babysitter), but it is important to actively listen. Experience will teach you where the line is. When a person feels heard, they are able to feel respected. Respecting others is essential in gaining their respect.

Be slow to criticize, and be sure to do it in private. If you are challenged in front of others, take it to the office. If you need to talk to an employee about their work, take it to the office. Don't let them dodge the issue by deflecting the focus onto insignificant things that are not the prime topic. You have to maintain control. You do not, however, have to act like an a**. Let them speak their mind; don't get sucked into an argument; know when to speak and when to shut it. If their mistake was really because of something you should have done or could have prevented, make sure you act accordingly. If it was their screw up, you still have to treat them with respect. Be firm, yet compassionate. Respect confidentiality. You are in charge, but treating people the way you would like to be treated, if the situation was reversed, is how you earn their respect.

Eventually that person will leave the office, and gossip will start up. The people who weren't party to what happened will still see how you handled it. They will still see the ramifications of it. Not only will you have solved the issue, but you will have created a stronger influence in your domain. People respond not only to the way you treat them but also how they see you treating others. If they can see that you acted with integrity, their respect for you will grow.

A leader is fair. You must be consistent in dealing with subordinates, and you cannot play favorites. Yes, there are some workers who are easier to get along with than others, some who are more productive than others; but they should all feel that they are equal in your eyes. Arrogance alienates people, creates enemies, and has no place in a professional working environment. Treat employees as professionals. They will live up to or down to your expectations.

A leader has courage. Have the guts to ask your employees' opinion when it is appropriate. They can often speak for a majority of the people in the office or on the shift. Again, this makes your employees feel heard and valued. If you value their opinion, they will be more likely to value yours. They will be more likely to follow directives without asking a million questions. It makes for a much smoother workday, especially those days that have a lot going on, the big boss is in town, or there is some kind of deadline. Which, if you heeded much of the advice in this book, should not be too much different than any other day.

Leaders support their employees any way they can. Some days it will just be about checking in with them to see how they're doing on their projects. Some days you'll have to get your hands dirty. You may have to jump in on a field survey, work on a presentation, or bus a table. Some people believe that bad managers hide in plain sight, working alongside their crew, because they can't manage their people well. You have to be wise enough to know when you are truly supporting your team and when you are enabling them to not do their jobs. You may have to make decisions on the fly and follow through with it instead of deferring until someone in higher management can be consulted. You should also know that sometimes it is better to ask forgiveness than permission. Remember, you need to lead the charge, not crack the whip.

If you've done all of the above, your workers should now feel comfortable enough with you to let you stop in at group BS sessions without halting quickly and pretending to go back to work. If you visit for a few minutes before going back to whatever you were doing and expect them to do the same, you send a good message and further developed a team attitude and relaxed working environment. Make sure that you don't get taken in by gossip. You can observe all employees simply by taking note of them during the shift. It's easy to overlook your best employees simply because they don't make any waves. Usually the focus is on employees who need watching or guidance. Make sure you stop to give some kind of appreciation to the ones who don't require your constant attention. Keep in mind that most communication is nonverbal. Watch for body language cues when speaking with someone or observing your workers.

Know your people. Find out why your people do what they do. It's important to consider generation orientation. The different generations see things differently, and it's important to be aware of that. You also have to know if the worker is a "face" or if they are a "workhorse." Do they love interacting with the customers or other departments, or are they quiet, preferring to work alone? Are they generally a can-do type of person? Are they a whiner, or are they whining? Are they able to take compliments, or does it negatively affect their job performance? (Some people with very low self-esteem have difficulty accepting compliments.) Are they a slow or fast learner? Do they need special handling? Are they consistently positive or negative?

Knowing your employees is essential in leadership for two reasons. One, you have to know if they have a selfish streak or if they're having a selfish day. You have to know if they are clowning around or if they really don't know what they're doing. Is it a skill or a will issue? No employee knows better than what you've taught them. If they need to be taught, teach them. If they are unwilling to learn or unwilling to set aside their bad attitude or behavior, then you have to decide what your next course of action will be. You can move them or try to motivate them. If they are salvageable, then, by all means, salvage them. If not, then they need to go. Some people cannot be helped. People who are not willing to be team players are just an impediment to business and a drain on your other employees.

You have to know your workers as people as well. People, especially managers, spend more time with their "work family" than they do with their "regular family." It makes sense that there should be at least some degree of familiarity with their lives, tempered, of course, by the lines of professionalism between managers and employees. This is also true of the upper management and their lower rungs of management as well. Knowing whether they are married, single, or divorced; whether they have kids, pets, or both; whether watching tv or skydiving is their hobby shows interest and concern for them, and, at a base level, shows respect for them as a human being.

A friend of mine had the good luck to work for a company like the one I'm outlining for you. The upper level of management cared enough to know personal details about those in the lower levels of management. They knew their marital status, how many kids they had, about how old the kids were, any hobbies. They could ask intelligent and caring personal questions that made the employees feel like they mattered. The upper levels of management knew most of the hourly employees' names as well. The cohesion, the unity, created by this was incredible. It was an amazing company to work for. The respect those in upper management had for all their employees fostered respect throughout the ranks.

The second reason knowing your people is so important? Knowing your people is necessary when you start to build your team. Team building is an essential, overlooked, and underrated part of being a leader. No professional football coach says, "Well, the draft doesn't matter. Just give me whoever." A true leader doesn't say that either. They get to know the people they have, so they can match those people to the jobs best suited for them, to the jobs that capture their interest and focus. When people are in the jobs that fit them the best, they are more productive. Then you are able to find out what your staffing needs truly are. With a little reshuffling, you may find that you don't actually need to hire anyone. The fewer you have to hire, the more money stays on the bottom line. You may find out that you do need to hire, but you'll know if you need a running back or a quarterback and hire accordingly.

There will be some people on your team who are there because of their positive attitude and their ability to raise the morale of the rest of the group, rather than because they have any impressive skill. There will be some people on your team specifically because they work hard and are efficient. There will be some people on the team who are there to be leaders and maximize the efficiency of the others. There will be some followers who get things done. There will be some who are quick and intelligent, able to come up with creative solutions to problems. You need them all to be truly successful. A great leader hires and evaluates people based on the company's, and the team's, needs.

Get your team to think about their job as if they were working for themselves. This can feel a little dangerous and requires courage. Encouraging people to make decisions and take initiative can seem like it could lead to trouble. That's true. It could. If! If you hadn't already done the work to select your people, train them up, and teach them to work as a team. If they make a small decision that doesn't work out, just go over it with them. More than likely, they will not make that mistake, or one similar to it, again. You will be able to handle them loosely because they will be taking responsibility for their work and their environment. Out of respect, they'll inform you of any necessary details and won't hoard information. They know that only pulls down the team.

Set your standards high, albeit realistically, for a group like this, and they will meet them. Most people don't realize how much potential is in the workers underneath them. They just don't see it because they haven't looked. Most people are capable of more than others realize, very often including themselves and the people who manage them. Encourage and help workers reach their potential. Huge dividends for all. Don't expect your workers to be able to sustain 100% output all the time. If you can get 70% output consistently, they will be far above average. In crunch time, though, they'll be able to give 150%. Allowing people to be people reduces the chance of burn out and losing your good workers.

With this type of team, you will almost never have to issues orders. If you ask, they'll get to it. Yes, there will be times when you, the captain, need to take over and make sure things get done in exactly a certain way. Most of the time, though, this kind of direction is unnecessary and even destructive. This will create a pleasant, relaxed atmosphere, one ideal for productive work. A good worker means you hired well. A happy worker means you're treating them well. A happy worker often makes a happy customer. A happy customer equals dollars on the bottom line.

A team like this will police themselves. They know when someone is having an off day, and the others will step up. If one is having a particularly good day, they will go to help one of the others when they are done. They are part of a team, and people love being part of something larger than themselves, working toward a common goal. It gives them a sense of purpose. There will be no need to micromanage such a team. In fact, you could leave them for hours, or even days, and things will be working just as efficiently as if you'd never left. You become a facilitator and support, the coach, as opposed to a "boss." You will be a friend, but, with this type of structure, the line between friend and "drinking buddy" will be well preserved.

This teamwork is the everyday job. It is achieved through people sharing experiences and having a common goal. The workers bond in such a way that the individuals subordinate their desire to the good of the team. Stated another way: it develops that the whole becomes more than the sum of the parts.

For this, leadership is essential. A leader has a concept of what needs to be achieved, whether that is to develop a product, support sales, improve shipping and handling, etc. The team is trained by the leader in such a way that the individuals become proficient at their individual jobs and become completely confident in their ability to do it in a far above average manner. At the same time, the leader encourages the group members to learn what other members do and how the different jobs all mesh to produce superior results. With little encouragement this type of team will always support each other.

Let's say the objective is to assemble an electro-mechanical product. Encourage the workers to learn each other's jobs. Say a rush order comes in, and the group has to work really fast but produce top quality. Watch, and you'll see that those who have quicker assemblies will start helping those who have more involved tasks that take longer. When the team comes to that stage, the output and quality will be superior to any group of box people. A real leader lets them know that they are superior. At this stage, you won't hear, "that's not my job." Also at this stage, you manage with a light hand.

Coming down from the top, you have to set the environment. Employees have to know that they are appreciated and trusted. Encourage interaction between departments. Building teamwork from the bottom up is an excellent way to achieve it company wide, and the work force will hardly be aware it is taking place. In fact, never mention it. (No slogans or signs posted on the bulletin boards preaching teamwork. Signs will tend to develop subconscious resistance in the individual employees.) Train managers to be leaders and promote teamwork in smaller, individual groups. While this is taking place, tear down the invisible walls between departments and encourage interaction and informed cooperation.

There are no easy recipes to build teamwork. This is where you separate the can-do people from the don't-do. True leaders understand the objective and find ways to make it happen.

Workplace tension all but disappears and the workers will become focused on "getting the job done" instead of trying to look busy eight hours a day. People will not worry so much about CYA, and they won't waste each other's time. Their respect for each other and their job will grow, making the work environment a productive and relaxed place.

Team building is not easy. Neither is maintaining the team. Conferences and such are important for your workers and/or managers to see each other in a non-work atmosphere and get to know each other better. You can chat, play games, have a short meeting. It doesn't really matter what you do as long as you're working together as a team, and it reinforces to everyone who their team is. This costs money and is often one of the first things to go in an economic downturn. It is actually even more important in tough times. You look at the people at the activity and think, "These coworkers are a great group." You don't want any of them to lose their job. You may not turn it into mental verbiage, but you are thinking it. What can I do to help keep that from happening? Seeing people as actual people with likes and dislikes, habits and preferences, and not just names (or numbers) can make a world of difference.

Not everyone wants to socialize with their fellow workers away from the job. For some, their family's needs limits or dictates outside of work activities. Some are introverts that need some "alone time" to stay balanced. Some will, and do, socialize with their teammates outside of work. Conferences and other team building activities should be done "at work." Said another way: make these work activities happen during work hours. That way there is no resistance in your team about the time they are spending. They are able to relax and focus on the team and the activities together.

This makes your team even stronger. This developing of the team will put money on the bottom line.

In addition to building and maintaining your team, you have to develop your team. Not just as the team itself but each member as an individual. This is where mentoring comes in. This is far above and beyond what most managers are willing to do or are even capable of doing. It is well worth the effort. At some point, poor managers squash the creativity and passion right out of their workers. If you can tap into it instead, you can hugely impact productivity. Good people don't work to a time clock. They are usually willing to spend the time and effort to learn new things, to do things right, to help out.

When you find exceptional people in your organization, encourage them. Point out their victories, their talents. There are many workers who are just that: they're workers. They just want to go to work, do their job, and go home. These people should be treated with respect. They are very productive but have no desire to move into managing. They are the backbone of the company. There are some people, though, who have the drive, the desire, and the potential to expand in their career. Developing employees like this is the greatest good for them and for the company. These workers will have more confidence, and it will show in their work. They will be less likely to make mistakes and more likely to stop and help someone in need of it.

An employee may outgrow their current role or position. That is a risk you take when you develop employees to reach their potential. Some will want to stay where they are feeling at home and valued. Some, however, will want to leave the nest. This is a difficult thing for a leader but also a beautiful thing. When it's time to let them go, so they can spread their wings, do so with grace. You won't find another just like them, but you will be able to develop another employee to fill their position, one who will do just fine. If you have the skills needed to build a team and develop your employees, you will always have the right workers.

Now, let's discuss why you would want to develop the skills of a true leader. As stated, it's hard work. People don't like change, and they don't want to change jobs. If the environment is bad enough, though, they will. It's a psychological fact that people need connection; they need to feel like others care. The manager, and the company, that has some conscience, and is able to fulfill their employees, to treat them respectfully and professionally will be the company with the lowest turnover. People leave people, not companies. Good employees will follow good managers. Contrary to popular belief, most employees are not inclined to leave or take advantage of a company if they are being treated well. Re-humanizing management and handling your people is a challenge, but done well, it is a company's source of success.

Leading your employees, instead of managing them, not only improves productivity. It also improves work environment. That improves employee morale. High employee morale reduces turnover. The cost savings in that alone is worth it. Turnover costs many companies dearly, and it is mostly avoidable. I had a good friend who sat down one day and did a little math, just for the fun of it. She was amazed at how poorly the employees in the company she worked for were treated, and she had seen many employees come and go. A rough estimate, after a few minutes of simple math, revealed that her company lost well over $2.5M a year in turnover. Two and a half million dollars! That's a significant number. Most of that was completely unnecessary. That company could save themselves over $2M a year by putting leaders into management, leaders who would raise employee morale by actually caring about their people, by treating them with respect.

"I don't micromanage." I have heard many mangers say that, and then I've watch them do that very thing. Not micromanaging is assigning a task to a person or group and not telling them how to do it. Leave them alone, and they'll figure it out, probably even better than you could. This builds self-confidence and self-reliance. It also frees up a manager's time so they can get their work done. After a while you'll start to see the changes. More work gets done, quality moves toward excellence, and the workers start loosening up. The next thing you'll notice are the smiles. Following that, often, is creativity. They'll come up with ideas to change a workplace so it's more efficient or different ways to improve a process, etc. Another benefit of teamwork is high quality decision-making. Team members will openly discuss problems. None of the members want to decide something that will embarrass the group. The result is far superior to the corporate model where workers are always trying to guess what the boss wants. The leader is a part of the team and is the facilitator. Even visitors will sense the enthusiasm of the workers. This is a great sales tool in itself.

Leading people, treating them with dignity and respect, inspiring them to be the best they can be, inspiring them to help you reach your vision for your company or department, taking the time to get to know them, working alongside them, creating kick-a** teams. All of these things inspire loyalty.

I understand that loyalty seems all touchy-feely and has no place in business. It absolutely does. Loyal employees work harder and more efficiently. Loyal employees have a higher morale. Loyal employees inspire new hires and turnover goes down. Loyal employees are willing to go the extra mile for their customers on behalf of their company. The fact is that every single one of those things adds to the bottom line. It's not a mushy gushy ideal that we talk about as we sit around the campfire, and it's not something that can be bought or sold. Only leaders can inspire such loyalty, and it is key in any strong company. Throughout every single layer and in every single department. It will add dollars to your bottom line and keep your company not only surviving but thriving for many years to come.

15: What it All Comes Down to

We've taken a journey through this book. We have taken a look at the corporate model—complex and terribly difficult to manage and keep profitable. Working on this book for many months, I've spent a lot of time thinking about these things and have come to the same conclusion again and again. Corporations, even very large ones, could operate very lean and efficiently, except for the human factor. When you look at most poor business decisions and follow them back to the source, you will normally find that they were based on emotions. Generally speaking, corporations are a jumble of emotionally based decisions. *Get emotions out of the decisions.* The criteria should always be how will this affect the bottom line? High employee morale puts money on the bottom line, and poor morale takes it off. Taking care of customers, regardless of the size of the company, is sound business, especially for the long haul.

Building a dynamic, profitable company requires including all employees in the business. Settle on a company focus and practice what you preach. If the customer is number one, keep everyone from the janitor to the CEO focused on that. Think long range. How do you want your company to be perceived today and twenty years from now? Partner with customers as much as possible by helping them stay profitable. Sell them what they need at a fair price.

Take care of customers, and the sales will take care of themselves. Go after profitable business. You can't stay survive just trading dollars. Be competitive on pricing, but don't aim to be the cheapest. Earn your prices by being the best.

Internally: treat your employees the way you would want to be treated. Encourage internal communications. Avoid compartmentalization. Train managers to lead, not boss. Assume workers are good, hardworking, responsible people. Most will live up to that standard and will be very productive. Do not attempt to micromanage from the top. Push decision making down line as far as possible. Let workers know they are appreciated as a group and as individuals. Aim for being the best paying employer in your business. You want any one of your employees to be worth two or three of any one of your competitor's employees. Avoid complicating jobs with petty rules and useless procedures. Tell your workers and managers what needs to be done and leave the "how" up to them. Keep layers of management to an absolute minimum.

The business should operate in such a way that if the CEO is not in town for several weeks, the company goes right on functioning at peak. Lower levels of management should run similarly. If a department manager is absent for two or even three weeks, it should have no ill effect. Good employees will know their jobs and what has to get done. Expect every employee to make sound decisions. When a supervisor will be away for a time, they simply appoint who will be in charge until they return. The fill-in shouldn't have to tell anyone how to do their normal work.

What if the CEO has a big ego and likes to feel important? If they are mature enough to know who they are, no problem. Follow the recommended management style and end up in charge of a dynamic $600M operation instead of a struggling $40M operation. I think I could feel a lot more important in charge of the bigger company.

Good management, good leadership, is good business. Running a business right puts minimum stress on any one employee including the top man. Everyone will come to work feeling like they count for something and are part of a great organization.

Your competition will always be trying to catch up to you. You will set the standard, and, as long as you run your company right, they can't match you.

As I've said briefly, a prime objection to this management style will be that you will have no control. Strangely enough, you will have more. Every employee will make it a point to let their supervisor know of anything important or unusual. That manager acts if it's needed, and they will decide what needs to be passed on up the management system. What the CEO will end up with is information that is properly evaluated, and they will know quickly about anything they should be aware of. What they won't be bothered with are things that are just everyday happenings in any company.

When a company operates the way I'm recommending, it's an amazing thing. Employees look forward to coming to work every morning. They operate in a positive, can-do environment, and they know they are part of a team. They know what the company is focused on, and they'll do their best to contribute to that goal.

When customers have problems, the appropriate people will act immediately and effectively. Problems will be viewed as opportunities.

A bar chart is one way to illustrate a properly (i.e. logically) run operation versus one operated based on emotional management. The bar graph below is hypothetical, but it serves well as a visual aid to illustrate the point.

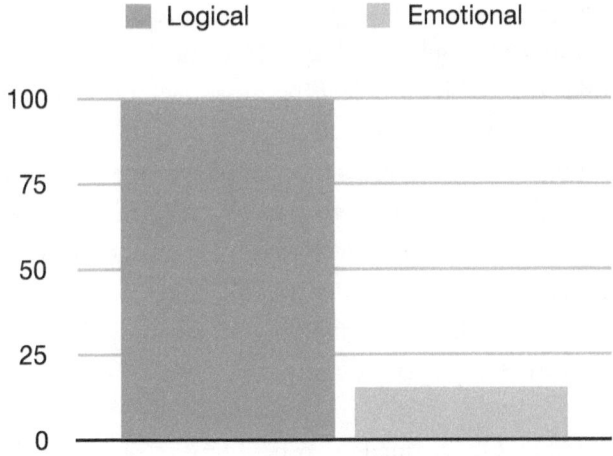

Creative Energy Available in a Company's Workforce

Logical: everyone is focused. Managers don't micro-manage.

Say your delivery people cover a whole state. Their first trip to a new location will be the shortest highway route. Then they'll visit with customers and also look at the map, and they'll try to find any shortcuts. It's not unusual on a 100 mile trip to be able to cut off 10-30 miles. Then, the driver tells his fellow drivers so they can do the same when they go to that destination. Over a period of years, this can add up to a huge economic gain.

Your mechanic makes a test instrument for the sales technicians. The tech department wants a second unit. The company is expanding so more units will be needed. The mechanic comes up with fixtures that will allow him to make the units in less than half the time it took for the first unit. That gives him more time to do other creative things and take care of his regular responsibilities.

Your company sells chemicals, and you have a new product that is 40% active material and 60% solvents. Working with the product in the field, they find that 20% activity will give just as good results. The unneeded 20% is basically wasted. The field man notifies the product manager, and they cut the activity to 20%. If it's a large volume product, the savings can be enormous. I know. I've done it.

R&D. Product development has to be populated with innovative thinkers. In a logical, high morale company, they can be amazing. Just try to tell them something can't be done. For safety reasons, you had better get off to the side and watch out. They'll bust their rears to prove it can. They will work hard to solve problems because it will help all their friends who make up the whole company.

These are examples, but, if you pay attention, you see these small things going on all the time when people are part of a team and morale is high.

Emotion driven: morale hits the bottom. Teamwork is discouraged. If a driver finds a shortcut, he keeps it to himself. There won't be any reward for telling others. In addition, withholding valuable information is a way to defy an oppressive employer. The employee doesn't think of it or define it, but it's there.

Your mechanic. Ok, he made two field units. Instead of finding an even better way to produce more, he simply tells his manager he doesn't have time to make more and keep up with his other responsibilities. The tech people can find a fabricator to make them for a few thousand dollars each. The problem is the tech people's budget won't allow it. The result is that the two units get hauled and shipped all over the country. Some salesmen who need the instrument may have to wait a month or more for it. In the meantime their prospect has found another company that has the equipment available immediately. That company gets the business.

The chemical that didn't need to be so strong. The field tech doesn't say anything to anyone.

The R&D people will produce innovations, but under an emotion-based management, the lack of enthusiasm in the company as a whole will affect them also. They will be somewhat isolated because communicating with other departments is not encouraged. Ideas from employees that could be of great benefit for the innovators won't be forthcoming.

Most of that 85% energy that doesn't benefit the emotion-driven company is burned up by employees trying to please the boss, not make mistakes, and subconsciously rebelling against their employer. People call this low morale, but few know what its origins are. The more rigid controls you have in a company, the more you choke the life out of it.

The 15% of energy that does benefit the company comes from a few employees who do the right thing in spite of management. They can't bring themselves to do illogical things and will occasionally defy company rules. Management never knows about it because those few employees tell no one. It would cost them their jobs. The vitality and energy gets sucked right out of the rigid company. It shows up on the bottom line or below it. In red ink.

In closing, this book is meant to open up people's minds. It is not a recipe book. Every day when I go to work, I expect the unexpected and adapt and adjust to it. Two years ago, I wouldn't have even thought of writing this book. I came to realize I'm an appropriate vehicle to do it. My objective is to help companies realize that there is a better way to operate so that everyone who follows the principles outlined here will be successful. It's not easy, but it is simple. It takes courage and vision. You can create a successful, powerhouse of a company. And I hope you will. Good luck to you.

Acknowledgements

This book is the result of input and assistance from a number of people. Essential to even getting the book started was my good friend and collaborator, Cindy Ali, and her daughter, Jennifer Brigham. Cindy and I met several years ago. She was very frustrated with the corporate world she was working in. Her goal was to teach good management in the restaurant business. My goal was to write a book on why corporations failed and how that failure could be avoided with good management practices. Her suggestions and insights were extremely valuable during the writing of this book. Jennifer contributed the skills she had learned from her own writing to help her mother and me.

The other people who made this book possible were all those in my life that added to my experience and knowledge. My family, friends, and work associates. Thank you all.

About the Author

HAROLD SMART grew up in a rural Oklahoma town and worked his way through college, serving a term in the U.S. Army. He graduated with a bachelor's degree in history with a minor in psychology from Kansas State College and also earned an MBA from the University of Central Oklahoma. He has worked with dozens of companies of all sizes over the last forty years and has carefully observed how successful ones differ from unsuccessful ones.

About the Author

HAROLD PRATT ...

www.ingramcontent.com/pod-product-compliance
Lightning Source LLC
Chambersburg PA
CBHW021956170526
45157CB00003B/1017